All Things Well

Deborah Sanford Smith

All Things Well

Copyright © 2016
Deborah Sanford Smith
Cover & Interior Design: TamikaINK.com
ISBN-13: 978-1533193148
LCCN: 2016907762
Cover Photo: JewelColePhotography.com
Printed in USA
All rights reserved. No part of this book may be reproduced or transmitted in any form or by any means without written permission from the author.

A Word of Thanks!

I want to thank my amazing family for being with me along every step of this journey. Words cannot do justice to the love you have shown me and the strength I get from each of you.

Haeley, you always came right back at me with scripture and helped me keep a Spirit driven perspective. Your faith has not wavered. You bless me with your confidence and trust in the Lord.

Arden, you never let me fall into self-pity. You always encouraged me and made me feel full of Faith & Hope. You have a matter of fact approach and if the Word says it, it must be, attitude. You cannot be shaken.

Joel, you always made me smile. I knew I could always rely on you to help my mood and bring joy in the room. I knew I could count on your prayers.

Ryan, you blessed me more than you'll ever know. Knowing that Arden had you to lean on during these days was such comfort. I knew she would hear Godly wisdom from you. You always encouraged me.

Dawn, my best friend. The cooking, cleaning, driving, and just listening are invaluable to me. Thank you for everything.

To all my family and friends who have brought food, ran errands, prayed for us all – thank you from the bottom of my heart.

But there is one who must be especially thanked, my hero, Jerry Smith. Jerry Smith, I could not travel this journey without you. I thank you for your selflessness and your unfailing love. You truly are a reflection of agape love. You are, indeed, my hero.

I'm writing this to shed some light on the plight of those who care for those they love. Many of us have been in this role at one time or another and others will find themselves there one day.

If you are caring for a loved one please know that although it can never be said enough or you may feel like it is never said at all, we know. We recognize your sacrifice. We see your labor and love and may you never feel taken advantage of. For those of you who are sick and are in need of extra care, please take time to appreciate your loved ones. Although it is not always easy to express gratitude in a situation you would rather not be in, please remember – your loved ones did not ask for this either. Please know they are doing the best they know how. They also have feelings, fear, weariness, and more. My story is about my care giver, but it is not to glorify him. My prayer is that we all realize that many more lives are affected by illness than the patient alone. There are many who should be recognized. Please take a moment to read this and let those you love and appreciate know it.

So, what about this caregiver?

Jerry has always loved me. He has always demonstrated his love toward me by the way in which he has served me – selflessly. He prefers me. No one should mistake his actions for weakness. It is quite the contrary. He is the strongest and most able leader I know. He is, in every aspect, the definition of the Biblical "Man of his house". He is not a push over. He loves me as Christ loves the church. So, when this diagnosis came in December of 2013 it was not a foreign idea for him to care for me. That part came quite naturally.

We had always shared many of the domestic duties simply because we did everything together and enjoyed spending every moment together. We figured we could help each other with our "chores" and they wouldn't seem like work so much as just being together. I did, however, take care of all the tasks that were administrative in nature, again, not because I controlled the purse, but because Jerry wanted me to. That was not his strong suit and he just really didn't want to deal with those things. Administration is my strong suit so there again this was a natural arrangement and has always worked well for us. We have never argued over money or business issues. I have always sought his direction for anything other than routine household operation and we have moved forward in agreement with any and all decisions. We had a system that worked for us. Each of us knew exactly what we did and how we did it and we always did it together. We had a great routine.

But there is nothing routine about a diagnosis that says you might not live through the week and if you do, your life will be forever changed. There is nothing routine about being active and alert one day and exhausted and feeling like your head is in a fog the next. Routine, what's that?

My life has changed, that much is obvious. I am restricted by limitations that I can neither ignore nor object to. I just cannot physically do what I once did (for right now). People call (very seldom now days with such Smartphones!), text, FB message, and email me words of encouragement and assurances of prayers. This lets me know I am on their mind. Everyone recognizes that I am going through a grueling ordeal. I have gotten a lot of attention; doctors, nurses, family, friends, church acquaintances, long lost friends, even the pets hang around a little closer! Our menu has changed to accommodate me. Our schedule has changed to revolve around me. Our family's budget has been devoured by me and my needs. ME ME ME ME!!!

So, what about this caregiver? Jerry. He is my knight in shining armor. He has never complained about being thrust into his new role. He has never complained about taking care of me. He has done things that he would have never imagined only a few shorts months ago. He has seen me in terrible pain. He has held me when I cried. He makes me laugh and holds me till I fall asleep. He is my hero.

But I know he hurts. I know he gets tired. I know some days he might want to run away. I know he carries our burdens. I know he wonders how we will make it, and feels like he can never do enough or get ahead. I know he must be scared at times. I know he longs for this to pass, but he never complains. He just does what he must.

Jerry goes to work each day to provide for our family. Many days he leaves me and he wonders how I will make it through the day. He worries that I won't drink enough water. He questions if I am lonely or anxious. His heart's desire is to be with me and care for me, but he has no choice, we have to have $$$. In fact, more now than ever in our lives. He buries his concerns and like all good husbands and fathers he goes to work. He pushes thoughts from his mind throughout the day and focuses on being a Godly provider. He has lost all satisfaction in a good day's work and just counts the hours until he can care for me. Before he leaves the house in the morning he makes certain I have everything I need for the day. He then prepares his own coffee and breakfast, packs his lunch and off he goes. Now that might not sound so awful, but you must remember – I was raised by a traditional, southern, country woman and was taught to take great care of the man of the house. I have almost always fixed his breakfast and packed his lunch. He has always come home to supper on the table and yes, I fix his plate nearly every single time the man eats. Now, he checks on me during the day when he can. His thoughts are never really his own anymore, they too are on ME.

After working all day he arrives home to start this second half of his day. I don't know how he does it.

He should come home to a clean house, supper on the stove, the smell of freshly baked chocolate chip cookies, and a wife anxiously awaiting his arrival. What he finds could not be further from the reality he once knew. Often times I am in bed. If not, I'm in the recliner in stained up, yucky pj's or a worn out Dallas Cowboy t-shirt! He can tell by looking at me what kind of day I've had and sometimes I know his heart breaks. He greets me EVERYDAY with a smile and a kiss and chit chat. Then he gets busy. He cleans the kitchen, takes out the trash, straightens up the house, and attends to my needs. After some time he tries to figure out what the evening meal will be. He knows nothing about this. He is willing to do anything, but he just absolutely knows nothing about cooking. Again, he is pressed into a situation that he did not ask for and certainly isn't crazy about. Yet, he has never said one negative word about this situation. This may be an easy fix for those of you who eat out often, but we do not. First of all we just love home cookin', but also eating out is costly and especially costly if we try to appease my dietary concerns. And remember, money is tighter than ever before right now.

It seems evenings are the worst time of day for me so I become more "needy" than ever. I need water. I need tissue. I need crackers. I need……. He takes care of all my needs. Then, after a long day of service he climbs in bed and insists on scratching my back until I fall asleep. Once I'm asleep he slips quietly out of bed and into his prayer closet. He knows he will do it all again tomorrow. He is my hero.

He takes me to nearly every doctor's appointment and is involved in every care decision. He listens to me express my fears and my hopes. He encourages me and pushes me. He has had to learn how to do some of the administration stuff and take care of all that stuff he doesn't like. On weekends he does all his duties such as yard work, miscellaneous little things that need attention and tackles the real house work of dusting, vacuuming, and all that stuff. He chauffeurs me everywhere I need to go and even makes the Walmart runs. He is still a father so he still tinkers on Arden's jeep and washes it because he wants to. He mows the neighbors' yards from time to time because he refuses to get "tunnel vision" and focus only on our needs. He still knows that it is far better to give than to receive. He still prays fervently for revival because he is a revivalist at heart. He prays for friends and family and people in foreign nations. He continues to do and to be all that God has for him to do and to be and yet he carries me and all of his new roles without complaint. He is my hero.

So, what about this caregiver? He deals with changes unimaginable. He deals with physical issues and emotional issues of his own and of mine. He deals with pressures of finances. He carries so much. Pray for him. Pray for him to feel loved and appreciated. Pray for him to have physical stamina and to be surrounded with friends and family who love and support him. Pray for his relationship with Christ to stay strong because this is where he draws his strength.

Table of Contents

Preface: The Journey Begins – Ignoring Vandal Hordes……….	1
Chapter One: The Journey Begins………………………………………	5
Chapter Two: The Journey Continues…..Waiting…………………	11
Chapter Three: God is in the Details…………………………………..	17
Chapter Four: I've Never Been one to, "Go Lightly."……………	21
Chapter Five: Nevertheless……………………………………………………..	29
Chapter Six: Jesus Equity………………………………………………………	37
Chapter Seven: Jesus Equity when Dealing with Cancer Patients………………………………………………………………………………	41
Chapter Eight: Inoperable, Incurable – Inexplicable………………	47
Chapter Nine: The Day I Lost My Hair…………………………………….	53
Chapter Ten: Have You Seen this Face?…………………………………	59
Chapter Eleven: When You Pray for People On Chemo………….	67
Chapter Twelve: Have I Cried? ……………………………………………	73
Chapter Thirteen: Just Because I Wear a Diaper Doesn't Mean I Have To Cry About It………………………………………………	79
Chapter Fourteen: When the Journey Gets Long…………………	83
Chapter Fifteen: Worship ………………………………………………………	87
Chapter Sixteen: God Changes Things…………………………………….	91
Chapter Seventeen: Trespassers be Gone ……………………………	95
Follow Up ………………………………………………………………………………	100
About the Author …………………………………………………………………	101

Preface

The Journey Begins – Ignoring Vandal Hordes

It is with great excitement that I embark on this experience with you all. It is my sincere hope that you will hear my heart as I share some of my life with you. I try to be as open and honest as possible with the hope that my experiences will bring encouragement to you.

My very first priority in life is to share Jesus Christ with everyone. My husband and I are both licensed and ordained ministers and have devoted ourselves entirely to sharing the Good News. Secondly, my desire is to see people live at the level of victory that Christ has already given to us. We do that by daily applying the Word and speaking life to our situations. I want to help guide people into the Presence of The Lord where real change takes place.

I pray as you share my journey with me – this journey of fear and faith, crisis and comfort, that you will be filled with hope, encouragement, steadfast and unshakable faith that will help you on your journey of life. The Lord has shown me many things throughout this journey and I know that many of them can help us all in everyday living. The truths of God's Word is strength for every day, regardless of the challenges we face.

Shall we begin?

The journey I am on right now officially began in October of 2013. The 18th day to be exact. That was the day we discovered a mass larger than a

PREFACE

grapefruit on my right ovary. I had not been feeling well for quite some time and decided to have an ultra sound after other tests yielded no information. I knew the day we left the diagnostic imaging office that we had a problem. We did not know what it was right then, but we knew it was serious. Considering my mother passed away in 2008 after a seven year battle with Ovarian Cancer, we felt like we had a good idea of what was going on. The 18th of October was a Friday, however, so we came home with little information and no facts. That was a weekend of crisis. My husband and I prayed and prayed and stilled our Spirits while we waited on real answers. The following week my primary care physician was out for the whole week so the wait continued. It was during this time of crisis that we began to feel the Comforter in a tangible way.

I will not bore you with all the details (at this time) of the next few weeks. It was in December that we received the official diagnosis of Stage IV Colorectal Cancer. After a week's stay in MD Anderson Cancer Hospital in Houston, TX we learned that the tumors had spread from the colon to both ovaries, the liver, and the Omentum (lining of the stomach). There is no medical cure. At that time I had a very large tumor in the colon and was 98% bowel obstructed. The doctors first suggested they remove that section of the colon so that my bowels did not rupture and cause serious infection and likely death. Due to the location of the tumor I would have to live with a colostomy bag for the rest of my life.

Jerry (my amazing husband) and I did not have a Peace about that option. I told the doctors that would not work for me because I have too much to do for the Kingdom and that would be a difficult hindrance in places like Africa and other third world countries. We asked them if we could sleep on it and talk again the next day. The following day, a God-send of a Christian doctor came in and we explained our dilemma to her. She got it! We decided to start chemo right away and pray it would very quickly reduce the tumor in the colon so that I could begin having bowel movements. I had not had one for many days. That is another story for another day, but you will love it.

A few days after that first dose of chemo I was sent home with still no bowel movement. My pain and nausea were being managed and the hope was that I would be more comfortable at home and progress would begin. Of course we were covering this issue with prayer and the Lord gave me Matthew 15:17 to stand on. Matthew 15:17, *Don't you see that whatever enters the mouth goes into the stomach and out of the body?* NIV. We claimed this verse and commanded the bowels to line up with the Word of God and do what they were designed to do. Two days later, yes, you guessed it; bowels began to work properly and have ever since. GLORY TO GOD!

It is important to note here that we value and respect the medical opinions and advice of our doctors. They are the best of the best and we are so grateful to have them (again another miracle story for later). However, as believers we trust and rely on the One who knows it all, the beginning from the ending. He holds the stars in His hands. He created us and He loves us. It is critically important that we take His advice and go with His plan in these times. We have discovered that with effective communication with our medical team that they understand our Faith and accept our decisions. We ask questions, very respectfully, and we take a leadership role in our care plans. No one knows your body like you do. Be involved. Do not be led like sheep by any other shepherd than the Good Shepherd. God has the final say.

2 Chronicles 20:15-30 The Lord will fight this battle. I love *The Message Translation* that says, *-God's Word: Don't be afraid; don't pay any mind to this vandal horde. This is God's war, not yours.* So that is exactly what I choose to do - **ignore vandal hordes**!! I will give no place to their attacks. I will live and not die and proclaim the works of the Lord according to Psalm 118:17.

Trust Him in all things. HE is well able. This was only one small way we have seen God in this journey. Just you wait, there is so so so much more!!

Chapter 1
The Journey Begins...

Each of us has a journey. Some may not be life-threatening or as challenging as others, but each journey is important. Your journey is your journey and it is the most important thing you have going on in your life.

It is critical that we know what God expects from us as we go through these journeys. My prayer is that through my journey you will see the Omniscient God. You will see His Sovereignty and His Goodness throughout every step. He did not just join my journey when the going got tough, He was there ahead of me making the way.

I have learned so much about God during this time. I have learned so much about His love and mercy. Today I can say I am thankful for this journey because without it I would not know God in the deep ways I do.

I want to give a little background information for those who may not know what is going on and just to lay a little ground work. My husband Jerry, our daughter Arden, and I returned home from Africa in 2012. When we left Africa after having lived there for nearly five years we were doing so in complete obedience to God. Our hearts and minds were not ready to leave. For goodness sakes, we had a lovely house, a vehicle, a great team of local people, and everything a missionary could want; but we declared long ago to allow God to have His way in our lives and just stay out of the way and OBEY!

When we went to Africa we went on one way tickets with only $150 to our name and one little Baptist church supporting us with $50 a month. We walked everywhere we went. We rode matatus (public transportation) with goats, chickens, and everything conceivable to go where we needed to go. We lived every moment of every day completely by faith. Some days we made meals from popcorn. We saw Arden lying nearly dead with malaria within the first four months of our stay there. We trusted God to heal her and He did.

We pioneered this work in Kenya. We labored and birthed this ministry with many trials and hardships. So at the time God said for us to return to the states we were not sure why or what exactly was going on. But since, as I said, we committed long ago to never get ahead of God but to always allow Him to run the ministry, we knew we had to leave. Fortunately for us, we had a little camp house at the lake that belonged to my three brothers and me since our mother passed away in 2008. We knew we could stay there and try to figure some things out.

So begins this current journey; and let me caution you up front, there are some topics in here that are gross, especially if you are not a medical person or that sort of stuff bothers you. There are some things in here that you have probably never heard people share openly, but it is my story. I have to share it.

Very soon after we settled in back here in the states I began feeling very bad. I did not think much of it at first because we had just made a huge international move, we had some uncertainties and other normal stresses of life that I could attribute stomach issues to. The dietary change alone could cause irregular bowels and all sorts of stomach complaints. So I ignored the situation for a while. When it became obvious the situation was not going away nor improving I knew I needed to see a doctor.

We tested for intestinal parasites and treated for all that good stuff just in case that was what we were dealing with. We even did a stool sample to check for whatever that does! The tests revealed nothing so we attributed it to a little of several things: the move, the dietary changes, the stresses of life, and just getting a little older and things changing in my body. I began to watch what I would eat a little closer and try to make some changes that were beneficial. This continued on for quite some time, many months. Before long though it was awful. I had diarrhea all the time. I had severe abdominal cramps and passed blood in my stool multiples times a week. I would wake up in the night in severe pain with what seemed like contractions for hours. I would stay in the bathroom for hours on end. I began vomiting frequently. If I managed to brush my teeth without vomiting it was a great day.

No one knew about any of this except for Jerry and myself. We prayed. We anointed me with oil. I sought prayer from believers at many altars. We believed God and trusted Him. And I got worse.

I remember one night in particular that we had gone to bed and I was in pain. I asked Jerry to just hold me until I fell asleep so he turned over to get behind me, in the spoon position. When he did his thighs slightly bumped my back side and I literally screamed out in pain. Needless to say, it scared us both because we could not imagine what could cause that kind of pain. There were many times that simply putting the soles of my feet on the floor sent pain radiating throughout my body; but we pressed on. We worked, we sought God about what He would have us do here in the states. We actively ministered and continued to live life.

One somewhat stressful thing that we were dealing with at the time was the issue of housing. We were staying at the little lake house at Dam-B, but that was not a permanent solution. It belonged to me along with my brothers so either we needed to buy them out of their shares or find some place to live. Honestly we could do neither. When we came home from Africa we came home to nothing. No savings, no 401K, nothing! We were starting from scratch and every little bit of income was going to simply live. So we sought God.

In our minds it would have been great if God had allowed us to buy out my brothers and live there forever. Of course we knew we would not physically be there forever but it would be a great home base that would allow us to do missions work all over the world, and yet have a place to always come home to. That sounded great to us, but it never got the go ahead from God. Now I will confess there were times I seriously considered asking for a loan to make this happen, but again – we committed to letting God lead so we never did that. This is going to be a very important part of this story a little later; remember this just never got a go from God. So, anyway, life was rolling right along. I had good days and bad days with regard to my health, but the bad were far beginning to outweigh the good.

So let us fast forward. October of 2013 is when all of this came to light. I was at the doctor again because things had gotten terribly bad. She sent me to Beaumont, TX for an ultrasound. Now you have to understand that at that time, we had no insurance and very little money so I asked the doctor to be very strategic and order the tests that would give us the most, "bang for our buck." We arrived at the imaging center at 6:30 on a Friday morning in October to have an abdominal ultrasound and a pelvic ultrasound. All the way there, Jerry and I prayed that we would get exactly the right technician and the tests would show everything that was going on. We prayed that nothing would be allowed to hide and we would have answers.

Now, here we go with GOD! As I was on the table about to start the tests, the technician started making small talk. She told us she had been doing this for 30 years. We discovered she was a Christian woman and we told her a little about what was going on. She then suggested that we not do a regular pelvic ultrasound, but an internal, vaginal ultrasound. She said we could see more clearly with that one and since we were paying up front we would get more, "bang for our buck." There was only one problem. It was 7:00 am on a Friday and she would have to have approval from my doctor's office to change the order. She suggested we wait in the lobby until 9:00 when the doctor's office opened or reschedule.

At that moment I had an idea. I asked her to hand me my phone. You see, I was friends on Facebook with the office administrator at my doctor's office. Yes, Facebook has some redeeming qualities. I messaged her and explained the situation to her. I gave her the technician's name and direct phone number and asked her to please call at once if she could. Within three minutes the phone rang and our orders were changed. Praise be to God because it was this very test that revealed a mass larger than a grapefruit on my right ovary. Because it was a Friday we knew we would not get any results until the following week, but when we left there that day I knew in my heart what we were facing. I cried on the way home because I just knew.

God is good, and He does all things well!

Chapter 2
The Journey Continues…..Waiting

The following week my doctor was out sick all week so we still had no results. During this time we prayed, we waited, we prayed, we waited. When she returned the next week she gave me the news. She said given my mother's history of Ovarian Cancer it seemed most likely that the mass was cancer and most likely Ovarian Cancer. She said the one mass on the right ovary was larger than a grapefruit. She was devastated. I can still remember her voice as she gave me the news. I began to assure her that everything would be alright. I let her know that God had me and that this news was no surprise to Him. I told her not to worry. I told her I did not have any idea what we would do, but I did know that God has it all figured out. That was all I had to go on. There have been many times in my life that I have said, "I don't know God, but I agree with You!" This was another one of those times.

Now let me interject some food for thought here. My mother passed away in 2008 after seven years of Ovarian Cancer. If you notice, the first thing spoken to me about the discovery of the mass on my ovary was Ovarian Cancer. The devil will always try to attack you first in your area of vulnerability. Given my family history this made sense to the doctors. However, I never accepted that. I rejected that immediately and said that I did not have to have what my mother had. I refused to take on that spirit of fear from past experiences. The Blood of Jesus runs through my veins and those things of old are dead. Right then I could have agreed and accepted cancer because it, "Runs in my family." NO, NO, NO! The *fact* is, cancer does run in my family. The TRUTH is – I am bought with the Blood of the Lamb and His blood cancels all those things. I hold onto the *truth*. The devil is a liar. He thought he had me with those scary words, but I know THE WORD!

My doctor's office began working on their end to get me in with an oncologist in Beaumont. They were fantastic. They called me frequently, but at this point we felt like all our hands were tied. I was not getting in with a doctor since we did not have insurance so we waited – again.

During this time of waiting I began to get some things settled in my Spirit. Please, do not despise periods of waiting. Ask God what He is teaching you. Ask Him what to do while you wait. I just worshiped and filled myself with the Word. This is of utmost importance because questions that are not given to God can lead to doubt and you cannot fight the fight of faith with any doubt. One thing I knew and am still convinced of is that cancer is of the devil, by the devil, and for the devil. It is evil. It is meant to take life. It is not from God.

God is good and the giver of life. I began to immediately declare, "I do not have cancer. This cancer is not mine. It belongs to the devil and will go back to him. This cancer is trespassing and cannot stay here."

When we face things in life, a good rule of thumb is to run situations through the lens of John 10:10.

"The thief comes only to steal and kill and destroy; I have come that they may have life, and have it to the full." This is from the enemy. For me it is simple: devil=bad and God=good.

Something you should also know is to never cast aspersions on God. Do not let the devil ever make you question the character and nature of God. The devil loves to make us have bad thoughts towards God. That is a victory for him. He loves to defame God. He is liar and the father of lies. You cannot effectively battle your enemy if you are uncertain of who he is. When sickness and evil come against you, call it evil and reject it and tell it to go back to where it came from. If I ever suspected that this was from God for even one moment how could I wholeheartedly reject it? No – my God is good. His loving-kindness is marvelous and tender. His love for me is everlasting. So I have never once declared MY cancer or I HAVE cancer. NO NO NO. This is not my cancer. It is of the devil, by the devil, and for the devil. It is trespassing and must leave and go back to where it came from in Jesus Mighty Name. It is not your diabetes or your depression or your anything. Send it back to Hell.

During this time of waiting I had a moment that changed everything. We must look for these moments because throughout our journey we will have to go back to them and stand on them boldly and use them to strengthen our faith. I was in the shower just minding my own business not thinking about my situation or anything in particular. I was singing and praising and completely out of the blue I heard in my Spirit, "This is not your battle. This battle belongs to the Lord."

So I said, out loud, right then and there, "Well then, if this is not my battle and this battle belongs to the Lord, WE WIN!"

Oh, Praise Jesus, WE WIN, WE WIN! I have held onto His words and continue to hang on to them today. There have been many times in severe pain and agony that I have wept in my bed and cried out to the Lord and asked Him to show up right then and there and fight for me. I have repeatedly claimed those words. I remind myself He is fighting. I force myself to not take up this battle because it is His and my victory is in Him.

Now you may be thinking that my faith must be incredible. That I am just an exception to the rule and that it is not realistic to be able to walk through such things like this. Let me assure you that nothing is further from the truth. I am no super saint. I have had moments of utter panic. I have cried. I have been scared. The enemy so bombarded my thoughts that I had visions of my funeral. I cried about maybe not getting to see Arden's wedding or Haeley's, or Arden's babies. I could not imagine leaving Jerry. I wept at the thought of how he would feel. But one thing I never did was question God. Jerry nor I have ever asked God why. We have not been angry at God. We do not feel as if this should not have come our way. The truth is we live in a fallen world. Good times and bad times come to the just and the unjust. Life happens.

One of the greatest desires of the enemy is to get you to question the character and nature of God. If

God is good, and He does all things well!

you begin to question then you open a door to doubt and unbelief. I have said many times and will continue to say, "God is good, and He does all things well." His character and nature are above reproach. One of the qualities of God is that He is JUSTICE. He is also fair. He is Sovereign. When we blame God for things the enemy does we miss His character.

I lived to know God. I want to know Him. I sang the song, "I want to know you more." When we know Him for who He truly is we can trust Him. Do not defame His name by blaming Him for things that happen in a fallen world due to the sin of man. He is good and He does *all things well*. All sin and corruption is because of the fall of man. Illness is a result of sin. Unlike Job's friends, we must recognize that it is not necessarily the sin of the individual, but rather, the fact that the consequences of sin affect us all while we live on this earth. None of us are exempt. The rain falls on the just and the unjust. How could we testify of a God who can carry us through every horrible trial if we never experience the trial? You do not receive the victor's crown without having experienced battle.

> God is good and He does all things well!

In a society where we pace in front of our microwaves and say, "hurry up," it is challenging to wait. We want to be active, to take action, and make things happen. We like to feel in control. I cannot tell you how many people have written to encourage me to fight, and I know their intentions and I truly appreciate it. For me each and every time I hear those words, I am reminded that this is not *my* battle, the battle belongs to the Lord. Yes, I have a part to play and that has challenges and difficulties that I must fight through, but I pray I allow the Lord to fight this fight on my behalf.

I began to seek the Lord about what my role in this is. I said, "Lord, if I am not fighting then what is my part? What would you have me do in this battle?"

The Lord revealed to me that my responsibility in this journey is to stay faithful and obedient. That is what I strive to do each and every day. Some days I do not feel faithful. Some days I wonder if I can do what He asks. It has been so amazing during these times of weakness that I can literally see His strength is perfect. I did not know that in such measure before. I am thankful for that.

Chapter 3
God is in the Details

So after weeks of getting nowhere with a doctor's appointment my pain level grew worse. On the advice of my doctor and a family friend, Jerry took me to the emergency room at MD Anderson. We prayed all the way there. At this point very few people knew what was going on because Haeley and Joel (my daughter and son-in-law) were in India and had no idea. We knew we needed the prayers of the saints but I was horrified at the idea of Haeley finding out via Facebook what was going on. I was determined that the enemy would not ruin their mission trip. So all the way to the hospital we are praying and trying to reach Haeley. We were successful with both. Again our prayer was that we would get exactly the right people in the ER.

It was incredible. Within 30 minutes or so we were in a room in the ER with an IV started with pain and nausea medication ordered. Our RN that night was a Christian woman from India who grew up only minutes from where Haeley and Joel and the mission team were ministering. She treated us like royalty and was kind and gentle. The ER doctor was a God send. She too was a Christian woman. As we began to share with her our life and love for Jesus she began to tell us about her recent mission trip to Uganda. She came in our room several times that night and took excellent care of me. She was moved with

God is good, and He does all things well!

compassion and worked diligently to get us accepted as patients at MD Anderson.

She casually mentioned to us that MD Anderson had a financial assistance program for people who live in counties that have no medical facilities. She said since MD Anderson is a University of TX hospital and receives grant money they help people in that situation.

During that visit to the ER they did a CT scan of the abdomen and confirmed the mass on the ovary. They also noted some other areas of concern, but suggested the gynecology department review my case since all assumptions were it was ovarian. The gynecology department came that very night and said they would accept me as a patient pending a tissue sample that proved it was indeed ovarian. Now we were in a catch 22. MD Anderson will not take you without an admitting doctor, and the doctor would not take me without a biopsy. This ER doctor then suggested that internal medicine accept me just for the interim to do the biopsy. Once we had a definitive diagnosis then I could be turned over to the appropriate department. She went above and beyond that night and we know it was because God ordained that she be our doctor that night. So once my pain was managed and things were under control we were discharged to wait again.

The following day the internal medicine doctor's office called and began working on my case. We began the process of filling out tons of paperwork and giving them every detail of our lives. A few days later she called and said they would accept me as a patient, but that I was not approved for their financial

ALL THINGS WELL

assistance program. I had an appointment the following day and that I would be responsible for the fee up front. She simply stated, "Tomorrow's appointment is $15,000." Well, it may as well have been $100,000. There was no way I would have $15,000 by the following day and that was for only one appointment.

Now this is where once again, I want you to see that God was already at work in this situation. Remember the ER doctor and her willingness to just sit and visit with us that night? I was reminded of our conversation and I told this lady I was now working with what I knew. You see, now we live in Hardin County. God had us miraculously sale the camp house in record time for cash in September and we moved to Silsbee, TX. There is no Oncology center. There is no hospital or ER or even a minor care facility in Hardin County (There is now, but it was not open in NOVEMBER.) If God had not sent the exact right ER doctor I would not have been armed with this arrow that made all the difference. This changed everything. Their grant provisions state that they accept people who live in counties with no medical facilities.

> *God is in the details! He was in the journey ahead of time!*

Also, remember how we just thought we must have that little lake house at Dam-B? That house is in Tyler County. Tyler County has a hospital. MD Anderson could have denied my financial assistance

God is good, and He does all things well!

based on that technicality. BUT GOD, in His Sovereignty and His great love and care for me MOVED US!!!! **God is in the details. He did not just join my journey when the going got tough, but He was there way ahead of me.** He is good and He does all things well. So, I told this woman that we live in a county that meets their qualifications. She said, "Oh, we didn't realize that," and put me on hold.

She came back on the phone and said she would call me back within the hour. Sure enough she did. She had met with the doctor and the office supervisor and they had accepted me for 100% financial assistance for an interim period. Praise Jesus. HIS ways are perfect! Very soon after that we had our appointment with the doctor, precisely the doctor that God had for us. He listened to every detail. He immediately rejected the idea that we were dealing with Ovarian Cancer. He ordered a litany of tests. He wanted to be very thorough. Jerry and I left his office feeling like we had a plan and someone who was on our side and would get things rolling. We were relieved. The dreaded words of Ovarian Cancer were lifted and the enemy could no longer use my mother's death as a tool of torment. God was working. After all, this was His battle.

We left MD Anderson that day with a plan and felt like we were making progress. The doctor wanted to do a biopsy of the liver because the other areas were too high risk. He wanted to determine the exact type of cancer we were dealing with. In addition to the biopsy, he ordered a colonoscopy.

God is good, and He does all things well!

Chapter 4
I've Never Been One to, "Go Lightly."

Colonoscopies are done routinely, generally, they are not a big deal. This was to be an outpatient procedure. It is done all the time without incident and was supposed to be completely uneventful. Jerry made me watch the Jeff Foxworthy video on YouTube just to get me good and ready. Everyone I talked to said how awful the stuff you have to drink is; which by the way is called, "GO LIGHTLY!" What a crazy joke – GO LIGHTLY. I was told I would be literally running to the bathroom. Considering how awful my stomach issues had been I was not comfortable at all with this idea or the idea of being in a vehicle between my home and Houston once that started.

Jerry and I decided we would go to Houston the evening before the test and spend the night. I could start drinking the stuff and once it started working I could start GOING LIGHTLY at the hotel with no worries about travel. Praise God we did this! He has every detail figured out if we will just follow His guidance. I have never been one to go lightly! I knew deep down in me that this was not going to go well. You have to listen to the Spirit of God within you.

As soon as we got to the hotel I started drinking the Go Lightly. Hours later my cousin and my friend both called wanting to know if I was on the, "potty." (Yes, I have close friends and family!) NOTHING was happening. They had both gone through this procedure and assured me this was just not right. At midnight – NOTHING was happening. The next morning I began, as I was instructed, to drink the rest of this concoction, but still no bowel movement. Shortly after 8:00am I thought I would die. Seriously. I began vomiting and having excruciating pain all over. Within minutes I was lying in the bed shaking uncontrollably, vomiting violently, and sweating all over. I was literally screaming out in pain.

   I begged Jerry to just wrap me up in the hotel bed sheet, call an ambulance and get me to the hospital. I could not walk. I could not dress myself. I felt as if I was going into shock. Jerry was amazing. He was terrified, but he went and got our vehicle from parking and came back with a wheelchair the hotel had. He dressed me and put me in the chair. Within minutes he had me in the ER at MD Anderson. I shudder to think of how we would have managed if we had been in our home town over two hours away. Thank the Lord for His guidance and that still small voice in my Spirit. This started our seven day stay in the hospital from December 4 through the 11th.

   At this point we were very weak, physically, emotionally, mentally, and spiritually. Jerry honestly thought I might die. I did too. We felt like the breath was just knocked out of us. It seemed to be a series of blows, one after the other over the past six weeks. So often we did not even know how or what to pray. Jerry just cried to the Lord for Mercy. I just tried to quietly trust. When I look back on this time I am so grateful that Lord enabled me to be quiet. I could have spoken so many damaging words

God is good, and He does all things well!

during this time of uncertainty. The Lord, in His grace and love for me had me just stay quiet. I did not speak words of fear, doubt, disease, or death over my life. I just kept quiet. I did not have it in me just yet to boldly proclaim life so staying quiet was the best plan at the time.

We were weak. At times, neither of us had the strength to pray. Yes, missionaries, pastors, leaders, all people go through times of overwhelming circumstances and desperately need others. If it had not been for the prayers of the saints during this time we would have been much worse. We could literally feel their prayers. When we could not carry ourselves; our friends, family, and Christians all around the world were carrying us. Please do not ever think your prayers are meaningless. When you tell someone you are praying for them, please do it. Prayer transcends time, space, and location.

> *Prayer transcends time, space, and location*

The following days seemed almost like a blur. Events happened so quickly. Each day new information bombarded us. We received the news that we were dealing with Stage IV colorectal/sigmoid colon cancer. The tumors had spread to both ovaries, the liver, and the lining of the stomach. We also learned that I had a very large tumor in the colon that was causing me to be about 98% bowel obstructed. This was the reason that I was not GOING LIGHTLY or going at all for that matter. It was blow after blow after blow. We would process one bit of information and encourage ourselves only to discover something else a few hours later.

The team of doctors assembled. We were praying diligently that we would get the doctors that God had for us. The doctors agreed that the best course of action would be to do surgery and remove the section of the colon that was obstructed. The problem with that was because of where the tumor was located I would have to wear a colostomy bag for the rest of my life. There was no possibility of a re-section later. My first response to that was, "That does not work for me. That will not work in China or other third world places and I still have a lot of work to do."

I explained to the doctors that we are missionaries and we travel into places where the risk of infection is your biggest enemy and that scenario seemed too complicated for what we do. I was not prepared to do anything that would hinder the call of God on my life.

When circumstances arise in life please consider what God has already said to you. He had given us great vision for the work we do. We still had many places to go and share the Gospel. This circumstance was an attempt to hinder and prevent us from fulfilling the call of God on our lives. Immediately I knew the call of God was not a "maybe" but a definite so everything else had to support that.

We asked the doctors if we could think and pray about it overnight. They agreed and said we could wait until morning. The next morning another doctor came in and we began to chat. She was a Christian.

She was from India. Her parents were saved when she was a child by missionaries who were ministering in their village. She understood and personally valued the work we do and the call on our lives. Praise Jesus! It was her suggestion that we start chemo at once and see if that would begin to shrink the tumor in the colon rather than have surgery. This is exactly what we did and exactly what happened!

During this week at the hospital the Lord began to reveal so much to Jerry and I. This was the most valuable time so far during this journey. For days I could barely lift my head so God had my undivided attention. Up until this point, Jerry and I had been so consumed with this issue that we had developed tunnel vision. We focused solely on me, on my health, and my needs. We turned inward and all strength was given to me.

One day I went for an x-ray and the Lord began to speak. I began to see others. I saw people who were far worse off than me. I saw people who were shriveled and those who had looks of hopelessness on their faces. I was moved with compassion for these people. I began to pray from right there on that bed for these people. It was then that the Lord whispered to my spirit that once we focus on self we are operating contrary to the Gospel. The Gospel is all about others. The enemy would love for us to become self-consumed so we are no longer effective and useful. This revelation began to change everything. We repented. We could not allow circumstances to shift our focus. We had to be steadfast. Our focus had to remain on God rather than our circumstances or ourselves.

I began to ask God, "What is my purpose in this?" I needed to know that God would use this situation and I need to know what my role would be. I wanted to be faithful and obedient. He reminded me that was what He is looking for in this. He wanted me to be obedient to the Spirit and minister to others during this time. Keep doing the will of God. Do not let circumstances, regardless of how they look, keep you from doing what you do for God.

What liberty I felt as I began to pray for others. Slowly my focus shifted from myself and my problems. Once I was no longer entirely consumed with my problems they began to appear smaller in my mind. Oh yes, we had serious issues, but they did not have us! We understood that according to the doctors that I might not live through that week. Every day was hour by hour. Jerry and I decided that regardless of what was going on we were going to try our best, with the Grace of God to keep doing what He called us to do.

Jerry started visiting with the people in the rooms next to ours. He prayed with them. He sat with some people in the waiting room and helped them pass the time. We both prayed for the housekeeping people who came into my room. We spoke life to every doctor, nurse, assistant, lab technician, and anyone else who entered our room. We were making the enemy powerless in our lives. God was big. Change was happening, not in my health, but in our Spirits! We knew we were in for a journey that we knew nothing about. We knew we were about to face the most difficult time of our lives. We had seen the difficulties that my mother faced. We did not want to go down this road.

God is good, and He does all things well!

Chapter 5
Nevertheless...

We started chemo right away. I took my first treatment that week in the hospital. We waited for days but still no bowel movement. My doctor actually allowed us to come home and see how things would go. We came home on a Friday considered extremely high risk for complete bowel obstruction and possible rupture. I had a bowel movement the following Sunday and have never had a problem with that again since. (Matthew 15:17) Praise Jesus – WE WIN! WE WIN!

There are a few other things that happened during that hospital stay that you must hear about. One day, a CNA came in our room. He was a man who looked to be about 50 or so. He was also from India. His name was Joseph. He began visiting with Jerry. Many times Joseph would say, "My God," this, and "My God," that. So, finally Jerry asked him exactly who his God is since in India they have thousands of them. He said Jesus is His God and His Savior and Lord. All day Joseph would come in our room and talk about what a wonderful day it was and how good God is. He spread love and joy all the while changing bed pans and doing other not so nice tasks. God used Joseph to minister to us. He used Joseph to remind us about the good things. It brought us conviction and to repentance. We decided to focus on all the good.

The next day as I was seeking the Lord, He revealed another nugget of truth for my growth. He told me I have been kicking against the goads. He said I had yet to surrender this journey to Him. I had to get to my "nevertheless," moment. I honestly told Him that I was not there. I was resisting and fighting this diagnosis with everything in me. He was not saying that I should accept cancer. He was saying that I must surrender this JOURNEY to Him. It was then I realized how many times we speak words in ignorance. So many times in my life I had told the Lord I would do anything He asked me to do. I would go anywhere He wanted me to go. I had laid down my life and that of my family long ago, but yet here I was taking it back. We sing songs declaring we want to know God more, yet to know Him more we must experience Him in different situations. When situations arise we do not look for ways to know God, but complain about them. We want to be like Jesus, but He was persecuted, beaten, and KILLED. We do not want that, but we SAY we want to be like Jesus.

Words matter. Count the costs of your words. When trials come do not blame God. So much of what happens in our lives is a result of our words. These words could have been spoken in innocence, not necessarily in arrogance or in any bad way or with bad motives. Many times we speak words without giving them much thought, without counting the costs.

I did not want to go down this road. I did not want to submit to this journey. I was kicking and screaming against it. This was hard and I knew the difficulties ahead. I told the Lord I would get there, but for right then I was not there. I began to remember Jesus in the Garden of Gethsemane. He did not like the look of His journey either. He prayed that if the Lord could that He would take that cup from Him. He anguished in prayer. He cried, but the beautiful thing about that story is, He got to the place where He could honestly say, "Nevertheless – not my will, but thine."

> *Nevertheless Lord – not my will, but Thine.*

I knew I had to get to *my*, "Nevertheless." I prayed. I cried. I can honestly say, within a short time I got to the point that I could say, "Nevertheless, Lord – not my will, but Thine." As soon as I did that – everything within me shifted. I cannot explain it to you. It just simply shifted.

Now, remember that I made it clear at the beginning of this that this issue is of the devil, by the devil, and for the devil and now it seems I am saying it is God's will. Let me clarify. This issue is of the devil, by the devil, and for the devil. I reject cancer and call it evil. I command it to leave my body which is the temple of the Holy Ghost and go back to the pits of Hell. This can only be done by the Spirit of God. I have surrendered this battle to the Lord because He said it is His. I had to surrender this journey to God's will. I have to be willing to allow Him to be God through this journey. He will work this together for good because I love Him and I am called according to His purpose, but only after I allow His will in this journey and in my life. So, nevertheless Lord, not my will.

Housekeepers would come in our room, dietary people, CNAs, lab technicians and every other person who came asked us what was different about us. We shared our love for Jesus with every one of them. One girl said, "It smells like Christmas in here."

I explained to her that we celebrate Christmas as the manifest presence of Jesus on earth, His birth. So it was quite fitting for her to smell Christmas because before she came in we had just been praying and worshiping and had invited the Lord to come fill that room. She was in awe. She said she did not want to leave the room.

On the day that we were hoping we might get to leave we had a very interesting visitor. The doctors and nurses had been in and out all day and we were still unsure about being discharged. Jerry and I were both moving about in the room when all of a sudden our door opened and a young man walked in. We had never seen him before. He was in a suit and was very nice looking. As he walked in the room he just stopped, like he was shocked or taken aback. Then he asked, "Who are y'all?"

We just looked at him like, "Well, who are *you*?"

Then as if he read our faces he introduced himself as the chaplain of MD Anderson. Then he asked again, "Who are y'all? Y'all are different from the people I see here."

We just told him we are Jerry and Deborah and we love Jesus. He said he had never felt what he was feeling right then. He said he had been through seminary, is in church all the time and ministers full time at the hospital but had never felt the sincere presence of the Lord. We talked with him for a while. Of course, Jerry prophesied over his life and ministry and challenged him. About this time, my nurse came in so he stepped out. He asked if he could come back. We told him of course. My nurse told us we were being discharged so we started packing up.

A few minutes later our door just swung open and in ran an out of breath Chaplain. He was down the hall and heard we were being discharged. He said he could not dare let us leave without praying for him. He said, "I need what you have."

He bowed his head and we laid hands on him and prayed for him. He gave us his personal phone number and asked us to keep in touch. It was absolutely amazing. We have kept in touch. We have spoken to him on the phone since then and have also seen him a time or two on our visits to the hospital. God is just amazing!

Another significant thing that happened was one day my doctor came and began sharing about her marriage with us. We talked with her for a long time and encouraged her. Then she came to me and sat on my bed and bowed her head and allowed me to lay hands on her and pray for her. We prayed for God to bless her and her marriage and then also for her ministry through medicine. I then felt the Lord lead me to pray that she would see a real, verified miracle of God through this medical case.

We left the hospital that day with little change in my medical condition, but with great Hope in our Spirits. God used that week of tremendous stress and uncertainty to show Himself to us in a new and deeper way than we had ever known before. We were terrified only to be reassured. We were troubled only to be calmed with Perfect Peace. We were weak only to learn that it is in our weakness that His strength is made perfect. We still did not know how the journey would go, but we knew we would be able to make the journey. We once again were able to say, "I don't know God, but I agree with YOU!"

After being at home a couple of days I did, in fact, have a bowel movement. We knew God was working on our behalf. I returned to MD Anderson two weeks later and started a vigorous schedule of chemotherapy. I did chemo treatments every two weeks. I would get connected to the chemo on Wednesday and come home with it with a pump for a total of 46 hours. We would disconnect the chemo and flush the pump and remove the needle on Friday.

The chemo had its challenges and side effects but I have nothing to complain about. There have been times along this journey that I have been so sick I have laid in bed and wondered if I would wake up the next morning. During these times I remember the Word of the Lord. I have told the Lord, "You said this is not my fight. If this is not my fight then I need You to come and fight right now."

You must remember the word of the Lord. Decree and declare the word of the Lord. Stand on the Word. I have to remind myself that this is not about me. This journey is about reaching others, encouraging others, and showing GOD big in my life. If it was my way, I might would give up. I might choose a different path on the days that are too tough. Many times along this journey I have had to restate, "Nevertheless, Lord, not my will, but thine."

Chapter 6
Jesus Equity

Throughout this journey I have received cards and money and food and acts of love that have encouraged and strengthened me. If the Lord puts it on your heart to do something for someone, do it. They probably need it. There is no way for me to adequately express what these acts of kindness meant to me. Surely, the Lord has taken notice of every one of them and will bless those who have ministered to me with such love.

Many times Christians toss out phrases such as, "I am praying for you," or "God will not give you more than you can handle," or "Just have faith," "You are more than a conqueror," and "Cast your cares upon God." On and on, the list of overused and under demonstrated encouraging phrases go. We have all heard them. We have all said them. I do believe that most people are genuine in their encouragement when they say these things. I believe people have good intentions. People want to encourage one another and let one another know they care. However, many times, simply SAYING these words of wisdom to people is simply not enough.

When a man has fallen overboard into the sea and is about to drown, the people in the rescue boat do not simply shout, "Swim, Brother, swim!"

They must throw the man a float or jump in after him. There must be an action that helps to rescue someone in that desperate state. It is important that believers build Jesus equity. We must make deposits into people's lives.

During one visit we met a man and his wife. Their name is Christiansens. He was visibly sick. He looked about a few seconds from death, and he had just been diagnosed with Stage IV liver cancer. As we talked with him I asked him if he was a man of faith. He very quickly and strongly said, "NO."

I told him I draw all my strength from Jesus and could not imagine if I did not have a relationship with Him. We just visited on for a while and I encouraged him. I did not speak to him about Jesus anymore. As they were about to leave I simply told him that in the midnight hour all he had to do was call out to Jesus. He just smiled and thanked me and they left. We have prayed for them ever since and I prayed we would see them again. As God would have it, we saw them again several times.

> Build Jesus Equity. Make the Deposit

We were on the same chemotherapy schedule so we would see each other every two weeks. The last time I saw him he looked so good. We were able to visit briefly and encourage them. Each time we would see them along the way we continued to build Jesus equity by stopping and taking time to talk with them and listen. After some time my schedule changed slightly so we have not seen them again. I prayed that we see each other again but most importantly that we see each other in heaven.

Build Jesus equity. Take time to talk with people rather than toss out a phrase. Actually call someone and pray with them. Mail someone a card or a letter. So often people do not share Jesus with others because they feel like they do not know enough. People make excuses because they do not have a "calling" to be an evangelist or a preacher. The truth is, many people are lost and hurting. People are scared and frustrated. People face enormous challenges and someone simply praying for them can be life changing. A stranger who says, "I know you are having a hard time, but God loves you," can make all the difference.

You do not have to be the one who leads them to Jesus. You can be the one who shows them Jesus in everyday life. The Holy Spirit will draw them. Make a deposit. All you need is your own experience. Share HIM. Build Jesus equity.

God is good, and He does all things well!

Chapter 7
Jesus Equity When Dealing With Cancer Patients

There are some things that cancer patients are not going to tell you most of the time. I would expect this could be said of most people with serious or terminal illness.

I NEED HELP! Once I was diagnosed with a terminal or serious illness everything in my life began to change. I was learning what matters most and what means very little. I was facing challenges in every area of life: mental, emotional, physical, and spiritual. It would be impossible to deal with all of that alone. HELP IS NEEDED. It is not easy to admit to yourself, let alone everyone else, that you are no longer able to do all the things you have always done, most especially the simplest of tasks such as laundry, cooking, driving to the Post Office. Friends and family call and everyone will always end their conversation with, "Let me know what you need. I would love to help."

While we know this is a very sincere offer and we deeply appreciate it WE ARE RARELY GOING TO ASK FOR HELP!

I CANNOT DO THE THINGS I USED TO. I would love to go to the movies with you or have a fun day of shopping, but geez, that is hard to do these days. People with serious illness have days that they are so weak and find it difficult to walk from room to room. Some days simply getting a good breath is work. It is hard to admit that we think about where the nearest restroom is and how embarrassing that could be. It is awful to feel uncertain about yourself and lack confidence in yourself because you may have an emergency in public and cause a scene. Too hot weather is a problem. Too cold weather is a problem. So time and time again, we decline invitations that we would love to accept, but uncertainty wins. Please do not think we do not want to be with you; we just have to make some changes in day to day activities.

There are some practical things that you can do. You know they need help, so just show up and help. Help comes in all sorts of ways. Most people will not refuse you once you are there, but will put you off and politely decline if warned in advance. No one wants to feel as if they are a bother to others. There are a number of ways to help:

- **Clean something.** Find out when their doctor's appointment is and go to their house and clean something, anything large or small.
- **Go by their house and get their car and go put gas in it.** Seriously, this saves time and money.
- **While you are already at the pharmacy**, call and offer to pick up a prescription. You are there anyway so this is not too much extra trouble so they may accept.
- **Drop off food that can easily be warmed up**. Be sure you use dishes that do NOT need to be returned. They have enough on their minds. They may have dietary restrictions, but their family members do not. Their

family still loves good food and the patient will be relieved to know their family is not doing without simply because they might not be able to have certain things. Or just drop off random groceries. Shopping can be quite a chore.

- **Help their family.** Family members have picked up slack in every area, yet still have all their own obligations and duties. When you help them you help the entire situation. Relieving pressure in any area helps in all areas. This also frees up the care giver to tend to the patient better.
- **Help financially.** The expense of serious illness is incomprehensible. Once medical bills arrive in addition to the extra expense of traveling for appointments and hotels, the family will rarely do anything just for fun. Send them a gift card that can be used for meals, gas, and/or groceries. Those areas get severely cut back once all attention is focused on health care expenses. Consider something frivolous like a manicure or pedicure gift card, because most will put that off. That is a real treat, especially for ladies, and can make them feel better all over. Not only that, but for just a bit it gives them a chance to not feel like all attention is on being ill. One issue that I faced is the crazy fluctuation in weight gain and loss. Clothes are not only expensive, but to spend money on myself ONCE AGAIN, when all the money is going

towards me already is an awful feeling. A gift card for that purpose would be awesome. The holiday season is a challenge for families facing serious illness. It is not only emotionally stressful, but a big financial concern.
- **Help be an encouragement.** Mail a card; yes MAIL it. It amazes me how special I feel to get a card or letter in the mail. Something that is tangible and lets me know someone thought about me. Also, mail their spouses or children a card. Even grown children who live outside the home. The whole family is going through this. Talking on the phone can be a challenge when someone is short of breath so a text message is great. I got flowers twice in one week and I literally cried because I just knew that God was letting me know that He has people all over the place who are here for me. My neighbor kids have blessed me with colored butterfly cutout pictures, homemade bugs from pipe cleaners, balloons, and have even left little goody bags on my car for our road trips. It means more than we can ever adequately express.
- **Stop by for a visit.** YES, it is okay. People used to do it all the time before we got so technologically advanced. You do not have to stay long. Remember, seriously ill patients are not getting out much for anything other than medical appointments so a visit is nice. In fact, a surprise visit is best because if you call in advance most people are going to try

to clean something or get dressed nicer or do some other task that they should not be concerned with and try to prepare for your visit. JUST DO IT!
- **Be creative in ways to spend time together** and in ways to help them with these changes. Often times the patient has to stop doing things they have always done and are stuck with the challenge of finding new hobbies. During the times when going out is a challenge plan fun times at their home. Have a pizza delivered and drop off a Redbox movie. Stay and hang out if they are up to it.
- **Plan short trips close by** and assure them you can call it a day at any time. Remove all the stress. Be patient and flexible.
- **Do not be afraid to crawl up by their bed and hang out**. One day a friend showed up and had coffee and brought her devotional book and just read out loud to me…what a blessing.
- **Grab a deck of cards** and play a game of something simple, just help pass the days.
- If you extend an invitation to your house please assure them they can stay as long or short as they need to. You need to let them know you understand and recognize they might not be able to stay for long, but you would love for them to come anyway. Then please do not pout when they leave early.
- **Offer your vacation home for a couple of days.** They will feel comfortable in a home

setting and the change in scenery is amazingly helpful. We were blessed by a friend to stay at his lake house and came home feeling entirely refreshed.

The main thing to remember is that all of your efforts are for them and their families. Anything that can be done to help them in any area of their life during this time is a huge blessing. Do not expect thank you cards or praises from them. They are doing good at times to remember the day of the week. Please just know that you are a blessing and they are very grateful.

Chapter 8
Inoperable, Incurable – Inexplicable

At the end of January 2014 we repeated the CT scans and all the tests to see our progress after four chemo treatments. The following day we met with my oncologist to get the report. The only way to describe it is it was the worst news and the best news all at the same time. The doctor said the tumors in all areas were responding very favorably to the chemo. All the tumors were shrinking and significant progress was being made, even with regard to the ovaries which are typically the least likely to respond to this treatment. He was very pleased with the progress. So then we asked how long he thought I would have to stay on the chemo. It was then that he explained this particular cancer to us.

We were not at all prepared for the news he gave us that day. He explained to us that Stage IV Colorectal cancer is incurable. He told us that once you stop the chemo it comes back. He said this particular case is inoperable because in order to do surgery we would have to stop the chemo, and because of how widespread it was that stopping the chemo would leave too many areas untreated for too long. Surgery was not an option. He said at some point I may be able to take a maintenance plan of chemo, but would never live without chemo. I then asked him how long someone can live on chemo. He said not forever. The typical life span of a person with this type of cancer is about five years if everything goes well, but the quality of life is not very good.

At that point, Jerry asked him if he believes in miracles. He says it depends on what you call a miracle. He went on to share with us that he is Catholic and he has seen some miracles. He also told us that he is on the Board of Directors for the medical committee of Lourdes. This is completely independent of the church and is a medical and scientific based organization that reviews medical cases to see if a *valid and authentic* miracle has occurred. He said they are very strict and apply the toughest of standards to each case. The only way a miracle is declared is if there is absolutely nothing that can be done medically. He said it would have to be inexplicable. So, I asked him if this case would fall in that category. When he said, "Yes," I told him to be ready to present our case to his committee.

That day we heard three words, inoperable, incurable, INEXPLICABLE. As we were leaving the doctor's office we were walking over to the infusion department to get connected to the chemo. The first thing Jerry said was he felt like we just got the best news and the worst news all at the same time. I agreed and then we agreed that we would not say anything at all right then. Remember, words are powerful and creative. When you experience a blow or simply do not have a proper response, the best thing may be to stay quiet for a moment. We walked to the waiting room in silence. We sat for a while then I called my oldest daughter, Haeley.

God amazes me through my kids all the time. I told Haeley exactly what the doctor said. Her response was incredible. She said she did not feel like there was any bad news at all. She said the fact that medicine cannot do anything is actually good news because it sets the stage for God to do what only He can do. He will get all the credit and all the glory. I hung the phone up and cried right there in that waiting room because I was so humbled by the truth of the words my daughter spoke. I told Jerry what Haeley said. We sat in silence a while longer just praying.

When I spoke, I told Jerry what the Lord was speaking in my Spirit. The Lord reminded me of the three Hebrew children. Shadrach, Meshach, & Abednego were thrown into the fiery furnace. They should have died. The furnace was heated even seven times hotter than usual, but the Bible says that when they came out of it, they came out without even the smell of smoke on their clothes. The Lord said this fiery furnace I was in was just heated seven times hotter. No doubt about that, but He also said that when we came out of this we would come out of it without even a trace of it on us.

I began to get excited. Right then and there in that waiting room at MD Anderson I began to claim that word. Jerry and I both received that word even though nothing in the physical had changed. The diagnosis, the prognosis, neither had changed. What changed, once again, was our perspective after we allowed God to minister into us at our most vulnerable moment. We held onto that word. We hang onto that Word every day. Inoperable, Incurable – No INEXPLICABLE.

The devil tried to destroy us with that news that day. We could have grabbed the words inoperable or incurable, but we decided to get ahold of inexplicable! Within a short period of time I was praising God because of what I saw in my girls. God used that awful situation to show me how strong they are spiritually. I saw God in the lives of my girls that I would have never known existed. They are women of faith. They have a relationship with God that is sound and solid.

Along this journey I have learned things about myself. I know God in ways I never knew before. I know that I know that in my weakness, His strength is made perfect. I know of His love and His goodness like never before. I know that I can stand on His Word during the most difficult times and He always comes through. I appreciate His Mercy.

> In my weakness, His strength is made perfect

We did chemo every two weeks until October of 2015, with only a couple of breaks. The regiment became very tough. It had some crazy side effects. I tried to handle them one at a time and refused to allow them to dictate my life to me. I continued to remind myself that this body is not the boss of me. There were days that the journey seemed long. I did my very best to never complain. I honestly have nothing to complain about. God is so good to me. If He never does another thing for me, sending

His Son, Jesus to die for me is enough. He has redeemed me, Glory to God. He owes me nothing.

The day the doctors said that one mass was larger than a grapefruit I nearly panicked. I remember looking at my stomach and thinking that a grapefruit in there was HUGE. I was about to freak out when the Lord said, "Yes it is large. That is very big in there. Anything the size of a grapefruit inside of you is huge. But when you take that same thing and place it in MY HAND it is microscopic."

What is your grapefruit? What is the thing that is so large in your life right now? When you put that thing in the hand of our Creator, the Creator of the Universe it becomes microscopic.

Will you give Him your grapefruit today?

Chapter 9
The Day I Lost My Hair

Early in 2014, the doctors told me that there was a slight possibility that I would lose my hair, but that more than likely it would just thin a lot. Just as they said, it began to fall out by the hands full. At that time I had very long, very thick hair. I had been letting it grow for years and I had a reason; bear with me.

Several years ago when we lived in Kenya, our Kenyan daughter, Cynthia, loved to brush my hair. She had never seen Caucasian hair and loved the silky feel of it. Almost every day she would say, "Mama Jerry, may I brush your hair?"

Of course I always said, "Yes."

I loved it. Not only was it incredibly relaxing, but it was a special time for the two of us. We would visit and share secrets and spend time together, just the two of us. It became a time that both of us looked forward to. During one of our visits to the states I got my hair cut in a short, trendy style that I thought would be easier to manage with water rations and all the dirt of Africa. When we got back to Kenya as soon as Cynthia saw me she was crushed. She wanted to know where my hair went. I felt awful. I assured her it would grow back. After some time we moved back to the states. Amid the tears of leaving I assured them we would be back. I decided right then that I would not cut my hair until after we were back in Kenya and Cynthia could brush her Mama

Jerry's hair again. So I let it grow, and grow, and grow. It had gotten quite long at the time of the doctor's warning.

Sure enough, just as they said, it began to thin. It was unbelievable. I would be sitting in the recliner and look down and have hair everywhere. I would walk and it would fall out. Every time I touched my head I would have hands full of hair. It became troublesome. I was nervous about cooking and had to be sure I always had a bandana or cap on while in the kitchen. It just seemed gross and aggravating. One day, I decided that it would not be so overwhelming if it was shorter because there would not be so much of it everywhere. I knew I needed to cut it. But I also knew my goal. It had become a point of hope, an assurance that I would be together again with my girls in Kenya. I began to get upset. I began to feel like the devil was forcing me into a corner and if you know me that does not work for me. I was allowing this issue to cause me some stress. I was never worried about my looks or about anything from a vanity stand point. It was simply something that meant a lot to me and I did not want the enemy to be able to steal it.

One day I was reading my Bible, and the passage came to me about where Jesus *willingly* laid down His life. He made the choice. He took control of the situation. The devil did not force Him into anything. The devil did not win. Because Jesus was willing to give His life it could not be taken. Now, please do not get all sanctimonious on me. I know that my hair and the life of Jesus are vastly different and I would never equate the two. However, the principle is the same. *Once we get to a place where we can give something freely it can no longer be stolen.* I called my hair dresser that day. She cut my hair in a cute, stylish little cut that would not be so overwhelming and we mailed six strands of hair to an organization that makes wigs for people with cancer. Take that devil! What he meant for evil we turned right around and used for good. He could not take my hair because I willingly gave it! I was upset that Cynthia would not get to brush through it, but I was ok because I knew that we would be together again and a simple hair cut could not change that.

> Once we give something freely, it can no longer be stolen

I started a new chemo at the end of July. The doctors said this would be a tough one and would have some side effects that I had not dealt with before. They were very certain that I would lose all my hair. I had already dealt with the idea of losing my hair so I felt prepared for this issue.

I remember years ago learning that my mother would lose her hair. I cried. I was devastated. I felt so sorry for her. She was a lady. She got up every day and fixed her face and hair before she did anything, except make coffee. She was never vain or pretentious. She never tried to impress anyone. That was just who she was. She ironed her t-shirt before raking the yard. In my mind, her losing her hair would be catastrophic for her and I ached for her.

THE DAY I LOST MY HAIR

I will never forget it. She had gone some weeks earlier and gotten a wig. One day she came out with this wig on. Her hair was gone. No big announcement, no scene. I asked her all about it. For her, there was nothing to report. Little did I know that back in her day wigs were the thing and she was quite comfortable in wearing them. Now I knew why those Styrofoam heads were around the house when I was little. My mother handled this like a champ. She taught me a great lesson that day.

On August 7, 2014, two weeks to the day from the day I started the new chemo my hair fell out. And when I say fell out, I mean *fell out*. In less than three hours it was gone, except for a few strands that stayed around just to make me look like Einstein. It was incredible. I had to call Jerry at work and prepare him. I looked the same as always when he left that morning. Now, we would look like twins. The process of the hair falling out was a little unnerving because it is just so odd, but once it was complete I was ok. I looked a little goofy. I was worried about how my girls would feel. Would they be embarrassed?

When they first saw me they assured me it was no big deal. I am sure they had their own feelings about the matter, but they have never once made me feel bad. It took a little getting used to but I figured out what would work for me. Wigs, not so much. I am a cap person. I also learned to tie scarfs and bandanas. I decided to just be myself and not to sweat the small stuff. After all, hair is small stuff. It will grow back.

God is good, and He does all things well!

The next day, Jerry and I took a picture together with my new look. We just giggled at how much we looked alike. After 20 years of marriage we had begun to look like one another. We were both thankful that I looked like him and not Solomon, our Schnauzer. I know you have seen those pictures of people who look like their pets. Yea, those big eyebrows, mustache, and goatee would not work for me.

Throughout this journey there have been many situations that arise and attempt to affect my walk with Christ. Many circumstances try to steal my Joy and my Peace. Honestly, I did not always recognize that immediately. However, once I recognize what is going on and choose to crucify my flesh those situations become powerless in my life. I choose to look at every circumstance in the Light of God's Word. What does He say about it? I choose Life. I choose Joy. I choose Peace. I choose Jesus. One issue at a time. One bad report at a time. One sick day at a time. One awful side effect at a time. Jesus takes care of them all. If I can make Him the focus of my life I will not dwell on situations that are unpleasant.

When you focus on Him you see the beauty of Who He is! All things become beautiful through Him. That is His nature. He came so that we who are yucky and lost and defiled with sin and death could become beautiful, clean, saved, and filled with life. Oh that you would know Him today. Truly know Him and how He makes all things new.

God is good, and He does all things well!

By the way, in June 2014 we traveled to Kenya – short hair and all! God's promises are yes and amen!

Chapter 10
Have You Seen This Face?

In addition to losing all my hair, I had many other side effects. Some of which are not so bad, and others that are indescribably horrible. I have been so incredibly blessed. For the most part, I have had a relatively easy time in dealing with side effects. Until this….this face. Oh my word. I honestly do not even know where to start.

In November 2014, my doctor at MD Anderson informed me that according to the recent CT scans that the chemotherapy we were using was having great success with regard to the colon, liver, and stomach. However, the ovaries were not only *not* responding favorably but were actually getting worse. The tumor on the right ovary was actually larger than when we started. It was his recommendation that we change treatments in the hopes of being more effective with the ovaries. Of course he educated us as much as possible about the treatment and then he said he needed to be certain that I understood one possible effect of the medication. It could cause an awful breakout on the face, neck, chest, and back. Naturally, it does not happen to everyone, but if it does occur it can be extreme. He gave me all the gory details.

At this point, his pharmacist came in to visit with us further. He also went over this terrifying scenario. Again, he made it clear that everyone does not react this way, but he had to be certain we understood the chance. The good news was that the breakout would not last the entire time and would lessen with each treatment. Also they assured me there would be no scarring or permanent damage. Before we left, the PA came in to be sure we had all we needed. She then asked if we were clear about the possible side effects and if we had any questions. We began to get the impression that this was a pretty big deal. We started the chemo that day.

Within days, I woke up and saw a monster in the mirror. I cannot even describe it to you adequately. If you can, picture 1000 small, white, puss filled pimples all over your face. There was not one spot of skin that was not covered. My face was literally swollen out an inch or so. I had sores in my ears, down my throat, all around my neck, in my scalp, my chest and back. It was excruciatingly painful. I could not touch my face at all. I would be sitting in the recliner and my face would begin to bleed. At night something as simple as the sheet brushing my skin would cause pain. Each morning I would wake up to blood stained sheets and pillow cases. We slept with a fan and even the air from that would hurt.

The best way I can describe my face to you was I looked like I had leprosy. It was gross, disgusting, and honestly frightening. Initially, there was no way at all I could go out of the house. This changed everything. Life came to a screeching halt. For me. Prior to this all of my issues were on the inside. I dealt with them. I could still get out a little and spend time with friends and keep my spirits up. I could still take care of my home even if my strength was limited. I could still do most anything if I planned properly and worked at a healthy pace. NOT NOW. It hurt to move.

I have to point out how amazing my family was during this time. I was certain my girls would be mortified. I just knew Arden would not want any of her friends to see this awfulness. She was, after all, a teen-aged girl. I was so wrong. Neither of my girls ever said a word to make me feel bad. In fact, they were very sympathetic. As this wore on, they never acted embarrassed to be seen with me and actually encouraged me to go out in spite of this condition. The only regret they had was that this had not happened earlier so that we could have scared some kids at Halloween! NOT REALLY. You have to laugh.

I stayed positive during this time because I was hopeful this would clear up in a few weeks. It did not. It got worse, much worse.

Our family had planned and paid for a trip to Disney World for Thanksgiving week. (This was a GOD BLESSING that I should share another time.) We had never been on vacation together as a whole family. We always do mission trips, but not just pure fun, unwind, no agenda, vacation. We all felt this was what we needed more than anything since my diagnosis. BUT – HAVE YOU SEEN THIS FACE?!

We decided we would go regardless. I continued to tell my body, "You are not the boss of me!"

I was determined that the enemy would not rob our family of a much needed vacation. So long as we were all together things would be fine. I reminded myself that I do not have a reputation and that this life is not about me. I would put away my shame and just go. I would accept the stares, the looks of repulsion, and deal with it. I would be with my family.

At this time, my face was at its worst. I had huge scabs all over and would bleed randomly for no reason at all. I could not open my mouth wide enough to eat. I had to break food with my hands and just poke it in my mouth. I decided I would wrap up with scarves when we were in public so that people would not throw up. I knew I could not go into a restaurant for any reason. We made the best of it.

Along the way we stopped at the outlet mall in Mississippi. I wrapped up and walked a bit. The kids shopped a little. We stopped to eat. The kids went in and had a quick meal. Jerry and I ate in the vehicle. It was perfectly ok. We made it work. No one complained. We had a fantastic week in Orlando and made some great memories. I was unable to do everything the kids did, but that was ok too. Jerry and I got some much needed rest and enjoyed the change in scenery and our time together. We grew together as a family that week. I am not in any pictures, but believe me, I was there.

February 2015, three months later and it was still an issue. It would improve, then get pretty bad again. So much for it not lasting long. On the positive side, the doctor says that such a severe reaction is usually indicative of a positive effect on the tumor. Obviously, my body was reacting to this medicine so we expected great results later in February.

I have learned a lot during this trial. Some good, some not so much. I have learned about myself, but

I have also learned about others. People can be mean. People can be hurtful. People can be down-right insensitive, self-centered, and thoughtless. I feel sorry for them. They have not hurt me at all throughout this. They have only revealed their own insecurities and shallowness. My heart has broken as I have thought of people with permanent disfigurements. Why do we look at people through such a narrow lens? I am the same person. My heart is no different, only my face. Yet, people who would have been eager to meet me look at me with disgust. People fear what they do not understand. Rather than simply talk to me about it with genuine care and concern people would stare and talk about me. Parents would move their children away from me as if I was nasty. It was truly eye opening. It was extremely difficult for Jerry to watch. He ached for me. He wanted to lash out at people for being so ugly to me. He never did. He learned also.

Kids are the best, most of them. One little girl asked me if I had a boo boo on my face. I answered, "Yes."

She said, "It's okay," as she gently touched me. She was so kind and sincere. She made me smile. I agreed with her. It is okay.

I tried to continue to do things along the way during this time. It was painful so that prevented me from doing some things, but for the most part, I refused to let this body be the boss of me. I caught myself wanting to stay at home and not get out much. It was just easier. The most challenging part was seeing people whom I had known forever and they not recognize me. It was not their fault. I looked really different. I had no hair and a face that looked like a recovering burn victim. I caught myself trying to avoid people, not for me, but for them. I did not want people to be uncomfortable or uneasy. How? How did I do it? It was not easy. There were days that I just wanted to scream and wanted all of this to go away. I had days that I was so tired. I had days that I could have easily stayed in bed and had a pity party. I looked in the mirror and saw a person I no longer even recognized. I cannot fathom how my husband continued to smile each time he saw me and how he could so sincerely tell me how beautiful I was. I felt like he should have been repulsed by the bumps and sores all over my upper body, but he was not. He loved me, unconditionally.

> Choose to remember the promises of God!

I reminded myself this was a season. Seasons change. They come and go. Sometimes our greatest challenge is to outlast. I determined to outlast this side effect, it would change. It would go. I had much to learn during this time and I would try my best to focus on that. I would try to be a better person because of this and make sure God got the glory for what the enemy used to try to destroy me. When I felt the need to grumble I would be silent. I would outlast. I chose to remember the promises of the Lord. I would be grateful. I would rejoice. I would give thanks. I would cultivate an attitude of gratitude. I was learning, once again, and in a new way, "In ALL things, give thanks!"

Chapter 11
When You Pray for People on Chemo

After spending years of cultivating a life of prayer I have learned a few things. This chapter is just a simple FYI on how to pray specifically for people who are undergoing chemotherapy treatment. I am sure the lessons are beneficial in other areas of prayer as well.

Prayer is quite simply our communicating with our Heavenly Father regarding our needs and requests. However, prayer is also extremely powerful given that life and death are in the power of the tongue. We can speak life or we can speak death. We can speak faith or we can speak fear. We can beg or we can receive. I have learned to see prayer as weapon, if you will, that God gives us to use against our enemy, the devil. However, many times Christians just toss prayer out into a great abyss without planning or strategizing and consequently we do not see the results that we would like to see as quickly and as efficiently as we would like. If you fire an arrow at a target you will likely hit something, but maybe not the bull's eye. I want us to take a moment and aim our prayers so that we hit the mark and have an effective prayer life.

Now, before we go any further please let me say that I understand grace and I understand crying out, "Jesus," when you do not know what else to say. I believe in that and I do that. There have been many times all I have known to do is whisper His name.

God is good, and He does all things well!

He has never failed me. Please do not misunderstand me that there is some special, "formula," that I am teaching here. This is a lesson on developing prayers - mature, specific, intercessory, prayers.

> *Develop mature, specific, intercessory prayers*

Let me give you an example. I had been doing chemotherapy for over a year. We had seen the Hand of God throughout this time. We had seen some positive results and we had seen some places that were stubborn and resistant to the treatment. After many rounds of chemotherapy and various "cocktails," the doctor explained in more detail what was going on with the tumors on the ovaries. He explained to me that the ovaries are designed to prevent anything harmful from penetrating them and getting to the eggs that they hold. This is the way God designed them. He explained that other organs such as the liver, kidneys, etc. allow substances to pass through them because they were designed to do that. Therefore, the chemo would affect the liver and other places more easily than the ovaries. The ovaries were doing what God designed them to do. As he explained this to us I had a great sense of direction come over me. I felt like the Lord was giving me insight into how to pray. I knew then to take that arrow of prayer and aim it specifically for the target.

I began to share with my prayer partners what I learned. I asked that we all begin to pray that the ovaries would stop refusing the chemotherapy. I had had a partial hysterectomy in 1998, there was no need for my ovaries to protect anything. We began to decree and declare that the ovaries would stop resisting the chemotherapy. We commanded the ovaries to dry up and die because they no longer served the purpose for which they were intended. We had a strategy, a specific, and targeted prayer.

Chemotherapy is an interesting thing. I do not have the statistics regarding how many people are using this treatment but I am sure they are staggering. I dare say you can hardly meet a family today that has no experience in some fashion with these drugs. When you pray for people on chemotherapy there are some things to keep in mind.

First of all, please never, never, never pray generically that chemo do what it was designed to do. Chemo is a killer. It kills cells, good or bad. It does not discriminate. That is what it was designed to do. Pray that chemotherapy be guided by the Hand of God and go destroy every evil cell. Pray that it supernaturally not harm the good cells. Does this sound crazy? Perhaps. This is a miracle seeking prayer. This is a prayer that knows that God can do this. This is a prayer that wages an effective war over the plans of the enemy.

Next, pray against the awful side effects of chemo. The Bible teaches about binding and loosing. When you bind up something be sure you lose something. Pray against weakness. Bind it up. Loose energy and stamina. Pray against nausea and vomiting and give that person a calm stomach with a healthy appetite. Pray against neuropathy and tell the nerves to function properly. The point is, determine what the attack is and wage a strategic and effective war against it.

Third, please pray for the emotional well-being of the patient. Emotions are not as obvious as sudden hair loss or other more noticeable effects. Emotions can be concealed or even denied, but they are very real and have a significant impact on the health of the person. Often people say they are praying for me to have peace during this storm. I need peace. I appreciate that. Again, a more targeted prayer would be to pray about the things attempting to steal their peace: the stress of family members experiencing their journey, finances, fear, changes in daily life, etc. Call things out specifically so that your arrow hits the mark!

I could go on and on for quite some time along this train of thought, but I am sure you get the point. However, lastly, I will mention that when you pray for someone undergoing chemotherapy treatment that you pray specifically for their family members. Cancer not only affects the patient but those they love. So many times the family members are afraid to admit their fears and concerns because they feel the need to be strong for the patient. Pray that they too experience the love and comfort of God so they can be honest and deal with their feelings. Pray that they be able to be everything they need to be to the patient. Pray that the enemy not be allowed to plant seeds of bitterness between the patient and the family member. Remember, the patient is now getting almost all of the attention, the resources, and the time. Remember things have changed in this family and everyone has had to make sacrifices. Pray that the Lord move in all their lives in the way that only He can. Pray specifically for people to encourage and help these family members as they travel this journey.

Ephesians 6:10-18. *Finally, my brethren, be strong in the Lord and in the power of His might. Put on the whole armor of God, that you may be able to stand against the wiles of the devil. For we do not wrestle against flesh and blood, but against principalities, against powers, against the rulers of the darkness of this age,[c] against spiritual hosts of wickedness in the heavenly places. Therefore take up the whole armor of God, that you may be able to withstand in the evil day, and having done all, to stand. Stand therefore, having girded your waist with truth, having put on the breastplate of righteousness, and having shod your feet with the preparation of the gospel of peace; above all, taking the shield of faith with which you will be able to quench all the fiery darts of the wicked one. And take the helmet of salvation, and the sword of the Spirit, which is the word of God; praying always with all prayer and supplication in the Spirit, being watchful to this end with all perseverance and supplication for all the saints—*

The last weapon mentioned is prayer. Prayer directs the battle. Prayer wins!

Chapter 12
Have I Cried?

Have I cried? Seriously, have I cried? I am not made of stone and do not have a heart that is cold as ice. I have cried! I am flesh and blood. I am human. AND I am FEMALE. Yes, I have cried!

Jerry and I had a pastor when we were first married who made the most significant impact on our spiritual lives. He is retired now, but we still consider him our Pastor and spiritual father. He once preached a message titled, "Don't Camp at Cryland!" You can go there. You can cry. But you cannot stay there.

When we first received news of this diagnosis I cried. I cried because I knew some of the challenges that we would face. I cried because I thought of my girls and how they would be affected by this. I cried because I saw the look of terror in my husband's eyes. I cried because. I cried.

> You can cry, but you cannot stay there!

At times the pain has been so intense that tears come whether I want them to or not. At times, the test results have been so overwhelming that I have wondered if we could take it. I cried. One night in particular I was in excruciating pain and having very serious trouble breathing. We were at home and trying to go to bed. Jerry and I were having a conversation that no one ever wants to have. We had

God is good, and He does all things well!

some issues that had to be discussed because we honestly did not know if I would make it from one day to the next. On this night it seemed very possible that I would not. We cried.

God is not afraid of our tears. Tears are not a sign of weak faith. Tears are honest. Time and time again as hot tears have poured down my cheeks I have felt the sweet sense of the Lord wipe them from my face. Nothing is tenderer.

It is ok to cry. Just do not stay there. The Bible says that joy comes in the morning. After the cry, after the time of tears – joy comes. Let joy come. Let the truth of God's Word rise up in your situations and let JOY come.

One crying fit I had I blogged about. It was entitled, *My Christmas Tree Has No Topper and I'm Bawling About It – December 2014.* I will include it here so that we can look back on it now and laugh together.

My Christmas tree has no topper on it, still. I decorated it weeks ago when I was feeling well because that is what you have to do when you are ill. I must capitalize on the good days and make the most of them. I am realistic enough to know that there will be some days that I just cannot do too much and so I plan, I prepare, I organize and strategize. I knew I would be starting a new chemotherapy and that I would likely be out of commission for some days so I started the decorating process early. I was so proud of myself and my husband who lugged and tugged totes and never once complained. My kids pitched in and everyone did more than their fair share to get *this task done. Only one thing posed a problem, the tree topper. I have always had a star on the top of my tree. I want a star on top of my tree. I LIKE A STAR on top of my tree. I have a beautiful star that lights up. It will not, no matter how we try, go on top of this tree. I have accepted that and moved on. I actually decided to get this adorable snow man tree topper that I saw. (I collect snow men so this was a good alternative) That is as far as I have gotten. It is December 11th – tree has been up a while now – no tree topper.*

This morning I wake up and decide to bawl like a baby because my tree has no topper on it – no star – no snowman – no NOTHING!!!! I actually considered just taking the whole thing down. Crazy?? Yes – crazy! Absolutely crazy!!! I feel it in my brain – the craziness. Since I know that I am not actually a crazy person I sat myself right down and began to question myself. (Yes, I talk to myself often. Don't say that's crazy because I know everyone does!) I ask myself what is really going on. Why in the world would you cry over a tree topper? That just seems to be the straw that broke the camel's back. I began to tell myself all the things that make me want to cry today: my house is a disaster, I need to buy groceries, my face hurts, my body hurts, I would love to go do a little shopping but this face isn't going to let that happen, not to mention there is no money for that now, our vehicles need serious attention, Jerry's work has been slow, and on and on and on this conversation goes. I just get it all out.

God is good, and He does all things well!

HAVE I CRIED?

Now, don't pretend you've never had that moment. So at the conclusion of this self-talk I try to figure out the root of the issue.

*Accepting that you cannot do
what you've always done is hard.*

I am a real go-getter. I was. I could get up early, have my house spotless, run all my errands which includem buying groceries and necessities such as tree toppers, and have dinner started by noon. I did. Today I made me some toast by 10:00am. I checked my email. Accepting that you cannot do what you've always done is hard. I want to do things. I think about doing things. I have ideas. Then I remember that I can't do that right now. I have to accept that.

So, how do I handle it? How do I change the way I have always been? How do I find value in the day when I cannot do much to help my family and need *them* to take care of me so much? How do I pass an entire day without worrying about bills and Christmas and blah blah blah with so little to occupy my time? Why get up? Why bother? Surely I could just sleep until this passes, right?

Then I read my devotional. Right now I am reading, *Jesus Calling Enjoying Peace in His Presence* by Sarah Young. It says, "I am working on your behalf. Bring Me all your concerns, including your dreams. Talk with Me about everything, letting the Light of My Presence shine on your hopes and plans……..If you want to work with Me, you have to accept My time frame. Hurry is not in My nature. Abraham and Sarah had to wait many years for the

God is good, and He does all things well!

fulfillment of my promise, a son. How their long wait intensified their enjoyment of this child! Faith is the assurance of things hoped for, perceiving as real fact what is not revealed to the senses."

WOW – WOW – Thank you, Jesus! The Word of God brought me clarity and revelation today about *me*. In the physical sense I simply cannot do what I have always done. FOR NOW! This too shall pass. This is only a season. The Word of God reminded me that Faith requires me to hope for the things that are not YET seen. I got trapped by looking at things as they are right now. How easy it is to do that.

I realized I was looking too long and too hard at the physical. I allowed my focus to linger on the things that are not really all that important. For a moment I began to concern myself about myself. I do not want to put myself in that position. I decided long ago to lay my life down. I do not want to pick it up again. I do not want this journey to ever become about me. I only want to stay faithful and obedient. In order to do that I must keep my eyes in the Spirit. I will fix my eyes firmly on Jesus who is the Author and Finisher of my faith. I remember that He never leaves me nor forsakes me. The Word of God always heals me. You can find great strength and comfort in His Word.

I will accept this time as a time to do things differently than before. Rather than focus on what I can no longer do I will gladly do what I can. I can pray. I can study. I can worship. I can write. I can encourage. I can motivate. I can bless. I can draw closer to my Father. I can love. I can listen. I can. I can. I can.

So can you…………………..

2 Kings 6:17 And Elisha prayed, and said, *"Lord, I pray, open his eyes that he may see."*

I still don't have a tree topper – oh well, at least I'm not bawling about it. That would be crazy!! I still have moments that I cry. But now days, I cry because some sweet friend took time to mail me a card of encouragement. I cry because I see a child pick a flower in the yard and give to his Mama. I cry because my babies call from Kenya to tell me they are praying for me. I cry because my daughter turned 18 and is an amazing Godly woman. I cry because I see the Goodness of God in people and I am humbled and amazed at how He cares for us. I cry – tears of appreciation, tears of knowing, and tears of JOY. Joy comes!

Chapter 13
Just Because I Wear a Diaper Doesn't Mean I Have To Cry About It

Some days I think if we could all take a deep breath and GET OVER OURSELVES we would be doing ourselves a great favor. Seriously, so many people are tied up all in knots about so many things but when we take time to break them down we realize maybe life is not so bad after all.

Romans 12:3 For by the grace given me I say to every one of you. Do not think of yourself more highly than you ought, but rather think of yourself with sober judgment, in accordance with the measure of faith God has given you.

Many things have changed in my life since beginning this journey. I went from being a young 44 year old who could physically do anything I decided to do to a sometimes feeble 46 year old wearing an adult diaper. I know that shatters all of your visions of me as a vibrant, sexy, gorgeous female, but hey – it is what it is! When serious illness takes a toll on a body you experience things you never dreamt would come your way. With tumors larger than grapefruit are pressing and moving all sorts of internal organs around, things begin to malfunction and function differently than ever before.

What used to be a sneeze is now a major restroom emergency! Now days when I have to go I have to go NOW. Things change. I have learned I can attempt to fight those changes or I can embrace them, head on, and do what I have to do to manage them. I have learned that I can let these issues control me or I can control them. I can be embarrassed about where I am in life right now. I can feel sorry for myself – OR I can get over myself. I can choose to be thankful that I have options to manage these and all the other issues that come up. I can decide to focus on FAITH rather than failure.

> Focus On FAITH Rather than Failure!

God has given me the faith to get through this. If I allow myself to get into self-pity and fear then I am hardly exercising that faith. I have to think of myself through that lens of faith. The body says, "You cannot go out today because you may have an *issue*."

Faith, says, "I'll go anyway. I will manage my issue because I am an overcomer. I will not be controlled by this physical body."

Often times I tell my body, "Body, you are not the boss of me."

I am not a victim. I am victorious! I decided to just get over myself and deal with whatever I have to deal with. So, adult diapers are now neatly stored under the counter in my bathroom for the occasion that I might need them – BIG DEAL! Thank goodness for these things. I refuse to stop and pout and feel sorry for myself. I can put on my big girl adult diaper and continue to go about and do things without letting fear and uncertainty control me. The devil gets another black eye.

God is good, and He does all things well!

When we choose to look at ourselves and situations soberly, without worrying about our own appearance and our own reputation we can access situations more clearly. We must get over ourselves and realize God has given us the measure of faith we need for every circumstance. Today, choose FAITH!

Chapter 14
When the Journey Gets Long

How do you manage when the journey is so long? How do you eat an elephant? One bite at a time. Day by day. One day at a time. Often times, one hour at a time. One step at a time. All journeys begin with one step. One step.

I was "officially" diagnosed with Colorectal Cancer in December of 2013. I was sick for a very long time before that. I had been doing chemotherapy every two weeks for over two years with only a couple of small breaks. Some days, this journey seemed so long. Most of the days it was a challenge to do the things I needed to do to get through that day. It started with getting out of bed. Yes, some days that was the biggest obstacle I faced. Often times I did not have the energy to get to the bathroom alone.

My husband had to work. We were not born independently wealthy. We make it. So, I would be home alone throughout the week. After the bathroom I had to get something to eat. Eating was vitally important in order to build up any strength for the day. Nothing sounded good. It did not matter. Eat something. On good days I managed to brush my teeth, put on deodorant and sometimes even get dressed. There are times this journey seemed long.

Every two weeks we traveled to Houston for treatment. I usually felt pretty good a couple of days before this appointment. The roughest days of chemo are immediately following the treatment. I had about 4 days every two weeks that I actually felt fairly well. I would try to get as much done as possible during that time. I tried to cook and clean and bake and take my kid lunch to school and do all the things I should have been able to do all the time. I tried to pay bills and take care of ministry business while my head was somewhat clear of some of the chemo fog. I would try to get out a little, maybe go to a basketball game or have dinner out to simply remind myself that life goes on. In the back of my mind, however, I always knew in a few days it would start again. The journey was long.

My husband rarely had one full week of work. Every week, every check was short. He tried to work as much as possible, but that was impossible due to having to take care of me. We were so thankful he had a job that allowed him to be with me when it was necessary. He did all he could do, but most of the time it seemed it was just not quite enough. At that time, our daughter would soon be graduating high school with college right around the corner. All money was gone now because I needed to live. We had vehicles making it on a wing and a prayer and getting mile after mile added every week. We knew we would have to make vehicle changes very soon, but the idea of a monthly note with all the uncertainty and medical expense we faced was overwhelming. Oh, the journey – it was long.

How do you manage when the journey is so long? How do you eat an elephant? One bite at a time. Day by day. One day at a time. Often times, one hour at a time. One step at a time. All journeys begin with one step. One step.

In the gospel of Matthew, chapter 11 verses 28-30, Jesus tells us, *"Come to me all you who are weary and burdened, and I will give you rest. Take my yoke upon you and learn from me, for I am gentle and humble in heart, and you will find rest for your souls. For my yoke is easy and my burden is light."* NIV. In the Amplified version verse 28 says, *"...you who labor and are heavy-laden and overburdened, and I will cause you to rest. [I will ease and relieve and refresh your souls.]*

> *All Journeys begin with one step*

He was speaking to a crowd that was weighted down, burdened, carrying a heavy load of oppression. They had been exploited and condemned by a burdensome religious system. He wanted to free them. He wanted to take away their heavy load and connect them with Him. His way. His plan. He wanted them to attach themselves to Him so that He could give them rest.

Today, many of us are weighted down, burdened, and carrying heavy loads that were never ours to carry. Jesus wants to free us. In one study, I found the word, "heavy-laden," to mean, "long journey." A journey that leads to the grave.

Does your journey ever seem long? Jesus has a yoke. The Bible says it is easy. To be yoked with Jesus means to be inseparable. When we are yoked with our troubles, worries, illnesses, unbelief, sin, etc. we are unequally yoked and cannot move forward. We are quite literally being pulled in two different directions. We will not make much progress. The journey will be long. When Jesus says He will give you rest He is saying that He will recover your life. He will give you rest so that you can complete the mission! Rest so you have strength to go on!!

I choose His yoke. I choose to let Him carry my load. I choose His rest today so that I have strength to go on. I choose to complete my mission. One day at a time. One moment at a time. I literally say (out loud) as I am trying to get the out of the bed, "Jesus, I need you to help me. I need you to strengthen these legs and get me to the bathroom. I know we can do this together. I need you."

When my journey gets long I must realize I am trying to travel alone. I am trying to figure things out in my own head. I am trying to handle things in my own strength. I am trying to solve all the problems in one swoop. I have taken the yoke upon myself. I must recognize that I am getting ahead of myself. I have to stop. I have to take it all to Jesus. I have to let Him have it. I have to rest. He refreshes me. He gives me strength to go on.

I must complete this journey. I will complete this journey. No matter the length of the journey, I will travel it. I will take it one day at a time. One step at a time. One step........

Chapter 15
Worship

The only thing that has kept me along this way is Jesus. However, I want to share with you a little insight into my relationship with Christ that keeps me strong and keeps me going. The truth is – many people have a relationship with Christ but never know HOW to use it for strength and daily living. I speak with Christians all the time who are living below their level of victory. I want to share with you one of the things that I DO. Not what I say, but what I DO. A practical piece of advice that will transform your life if you will apply it. *WORSHIP*

In today's church, worship is gaining a lot of attention and people are spending more time focusing their attention and hopefully their hearts on the King of Kings. Churches are spending huge amounts of money for the best sound equipment, lights, singers, musicians and all sorts of bells and whistles to lead congregations into worship. I will confess, I LOVE a good worship service and have nothing against corporate worship that is full of life and energy and enthusiasm. And I want the people who are singing to have great voices. I do not enjoy services that sound like someone is killing a cat. However, if our worship is about the music, the song, the words, the feelings, the goosebumps, and all the other manifestations and not about Jesus we have simply had a nice concert. And as great as that might be, a concert will never change your life. And it will certainly not enable you to live victoriously day in and day out, especially when the journey gets tough. A commonly known scripture that people use to teach us how to worship is John 4:24. *"God is Spirit, and those who worship Him must worship in spirit and truth."* I have heard many messages preached about what it is to worship in spirit and in truth. But I want to focus on another critical component of this verse. The object of our worship. The text says those who worship HIM. WHO? Those who worship GOD. The most important component of worship is the OBJECT OF OUR WORSHIP – GOD. We have practiced the songs, the dance, the tongues, the music, the performance and all the yada yada to the point that often times we lose focus of the OBJECT.

> The object of our worship is GOD

This is the key to my daily success. The object of my worship is my God. I do not worship music, although I love it and use it to focus on my King. It must be all about Him. So this is how it works for me. I *choose* to worship. I choose to exalt God in every circumstance. This is real life. When the doctors came in the room in June of 2015 and told me I possibly had six to nine months to live or maybe a year or two, I felt like I had been hit right in the stomach with a bat. My first thought was, "You have to be kidding. There is no way. I am not going to have that."

Then my mind, because I am human, immediately went to my girls. I wondered how in the world we would share this report with them. Within a few moments we gathered our thoughts and steadied ourselves as we left that room. We dealt with the reality of the medical side of things. Soon though, we focused on GOD. We began to thank Him for being in control of all of this. We began to declare His goodness in all things. We began to focus our hearts and our minds on Him and exalt Him above this news, worshipping Him. You see, it is far more than a song.

Day in and day out I set my heart on God. Many nights when the pain is physically unbearable and the emotions are spiraling out of control I simply turn on my worship music and focus all my heart on God. With tears streaming down my face I will shout out loud how good He is to me. I will remind myself that He never fails. I will tell Him how much I love Him and remind myself that He loves me oh so much more. His love is perfect. I will focus all of my attention on Him, the object of my worship.

When I can worship my Father during these times the enemy has no power over me. I will not pretend to you that my pain instantly vanishes and my circumstances change every single time. That is just not true. However, they no longer have power over me. You see, when I worship God during the most difficult times it invites Him right into that situation. And regardless if the circumstances change or not, I am immediately at peace because *He* is with me.

God is good, and He does all things well!

WORSHIP

From the beginning, the enemy has sought to steal our affections from God. He uses lies, money, trickery, busy-ness, personal dreams and agendas, goals, children, spouses, illness, devastation and everything under the sun to get us to look at anything other than God. He knows when we live lives that WORSHIP God we will be able to live victoriously, in spite of the circumstances.

Today, focus your heart on God. Stop looking at everything around you. Look at the Father. Worship Him. Worship is a lifestyle. It will enable you to live above any circumstances. Worship God. Worship changes things.

Chapter 16
God Changes Things

Since this journey began in December of 2013, surgery had never been an option. We asked countless times and were always told the same thing, "You are not a candidate for surgery. It would be too dangerous and the rewards too small to justify it. You can never be off of chemo long enough to do surgery."

Nearly every appointment we had Jerry would ask, "Can we just go in and get the ovaries since they are the things causing such problems?"

Again and again the answer was always NO. The answer was so strongly NO that my case was never even presented to a surgical team. In September of 2015, I received a phone call and was informed that my doctor was no longer at MDA. My first reaction was a little apprehension. I really liked and respected my doctor. Within moments though, I had a complete change of heart about this sudden change. I decided that a new pair of eyes on my case could not be a bad thing. I decided to accept this as a positive development, adjusted my attitude, and went to meet my new doctor.

When we arrived at the new doctor's office we were blown away at how God is truly IN THE DETAILS! We met his nurse and enjoyed her. Then as we were waiting to see him, his PA entered our room. Much to our delight it was a PA who we had met with our previous doctor. She had filled in for a

PA who had to be out for several weeks so we already knew her. She recognized us right away. GO GOD – thanks for putting us at ease!

After she left the door opened and in walked the doctor's pharmacist. Again, we had dealt with him extensively with our previous doctor due to the awful reaction my face and skin had to the chemotherapy. He said he saw my name on the list and although he was not scheduled to see me that day he just had to come in and say, "hello," and see if we needed anything. He reviewed all my information. He asked about how my treatments in Beaumont were going. He just stayed with us for quite some time and made sure we were really ok. GOD IS IN THE DETAILS!

Our new doctor arrived and we immediately liked him. He was young. He was enthusiastic. He was engaged in all the latest studies and seemed genuinely interested in seeing me live. Within moments of our conversation he asked if he could present my case to a surgical team. Jerry nearly fell out of his seat. This doctor believed I was a great candidate for surgery. Of course we told him to proceed.

Within weeks I had an appointment for a colonoscopy. Yes, a colonoscopy, the very procedure I was supposed to never be able to have again. The surgeons reviewed my case and wanted to proceed so they wanted to be sure there were no surprises in the colon. We never had a clear picture of the colon once the original tumor was discovered in 2013. No one knew if there were other tumors in the colon or not.

Monday, October 26, 2015, I had the colonoscopy. The results state, "No evidence of residual tumor at all." PRAISE JESUS!! My colon is cancer free! The nurse said, "The only thing we see in your colon is a small amount of scar tissue from the surgery to remove the original tumor in the colon."

I told her I had never had any surgery. She stood there with her mouth hanging open and then said, "Well then, there is a small amount of scar tissue from where the original tumor was, however it was removed."

GO GOD! I had to laugh.

Only moments after we got home from that appointment the doctor's office called to see if we could return to MDA on Thursday of the same week for a consultation with the surgeon's office. Of course, that is what we did. They also stated that if we decided to proceed with surgery that it would be done the following Monday. They canceled my chemotherapy treatment for that week to be prepared in the event that we proceeded with surgery on Monday.

As our brains were whirling and thoughts flooded our minds we were overwhelmed. Surgery was no guarantee and there were great risks involved with doing it at all. But we knew this development was a God thing. The doctors had always said inoperable, but God said trespassers would be gone. We knew this was only happening because God makes a way where there seems to be no way. It just amazed us at how God is so involved in every detail of our lives. He is always ahead of us. We cannot walk into a situation that He has not already figured out. God changes things.

Chapter 17
Trespassers Be Gone

The doctors were amazed and kept commenting at how remarkable this whole case was. The surgeon said I should have not lived based on the condition of my liver when we received the original diagnosis years ago. That was why surgery was never an option. We finally realized I was not a good candidate for much of anything because they thought I would not make it. Since my progress has been so "remarkable" and I am still alive over two years later they decided it was time to get rid of the ovaries and the huge tumors there.

The surgery was a HUGE surgery and required a very large incision. The surgeon removed both ovaries. The right side had a tumor the size of a football with it and the left side had a tumor larger than a softball. There were a couple of other issues that had to be dealt with, but the surgery was a tremendous success. That very day I was up sitting in the chair. The next day I was walking the halls. I was discharged three days later and have had no trouble whatsoever. I have not taken any pain meds. In fact, while in the hospital the nurses kept asking me if I was aware I had a pump that I could press for pain medication. I simply did not need it. God continues to be my strength!

The surgeon told us that he is amazed at how the liver looked during surgery. The official report stated there were a few spots remaining on the liver.

God is good, and He does all things well!

A few! This was the liver that was completely covered inside and should not have even been functioning.

Six weeks after the surgery we got the latest update on my condition. After surgery on November 9th to remove the tumors from the ovaries, one the size of a football and the other larger than a softball, we repeated all the scans and various tests to restage and set a plan of care. The news was not exactly what we wanted to hear.

Please hear me when I tell you to not let the enemy use your very own mouth against you. When we get reports that do not agree with our Spirits it is best to use wisdom and not allow those reports to take root in our minds and lives. When we accept those things and begin to repeat them and dwell on them we give them power. So, I waited and asked the Lord to tell me *His* report on where we were. I knew all along that His report is GOOD and we believed that so I needed Him to clarify this for me and give me specific details rather than a general, "report of the Lord," thing.

The doctor first told me that he believed we did a good thing by doing the surgery. He then went on to say that he was not sure that we increased the length of my life at all, but that he felt we improved the quality of my life for the time that I have left. There were a few tumors on the liver that were there prior to surgery. They had grown since I had not had chemotherapy since October, but they have only grown very little. He felt this was good news because that indicates to him that these tumors are not necessarily aggressive since it had been so long without chemo. Then he told us that there were two new spots on the stomach and two new spots in the right lung that had not been there before. This was difficult to hear. We were not expecting new growth especially into organs that had never been involved before. Again, he said they were very small and considering the length of time since chemo that was positive.

We agreed that because I was feeling so amazing that we would not restart chemo at that time. Due to the size of the tumors we decided to monitor them very closely and see what would happen. That was excellent news in my opinion because the chemo was becoming increasingly more difficult to tolerate and my overall health was beginning to feel like it was changing drastically.

We went to that appointment fully intending to hear that EVERYTHING was gone! We just so desperately wanted to be at the end of this journey. Our flesh is weak. It was upsetting to hear otherwise. My first thought was, "How will I tell my family?"

I know they are tired too. This journey has consumed all of our time, energy, and finances. They have worked so hard, sacrificed and done without so much because of it. And it goes on......

Again, Jerry and I did not speak as we left the hospital. We had to allow God to speak to us! In the truck on the way home the Lord said to my Spirit, "I am the Author and the Finisher of your faith."

So, I asked Him to explain that to me and He showed me a couple of pictures in my mind's eye. First of all, when something is FINISHED it is more than complete. I think we think of the finisher of our faith as someone who makes our faith complete, but there is more than that. Anyone can build cabinets and install them in a house. But a FINISHING carpenter can design them to perfection. He adds all the details, the trim work, and smooths out all the rough and imperfect places. You could have complete cabinets but not necessarily FINISHED cabinets. He also showed me a paint job on a car. The FINISH is that bright, shiny, perfectly done coat that allows you to see your reflection in it. Many people can paint a car. Not many can get you that perfect shine that reflects so much beauty.

> The finisher brings our faith to maturity & perfection

So, I began to understand the stage of the journey we are on now. The FINISHING - not that it will end soon, but that the details are being worked on, the beauty is coming forth. Once the Lord ministered to me about this I was able to bear it. I thanked Him for His Grace and His Goodness and told Him I will try to stay faithful and obedient. I will try to walk this journey with honor and with joy, regardless of the process or the outcome. This has never been about me and I do not intend to make it so now.

Hebrews 12:1-2 *"Therefore we also, since we are surrounded by so great a cloud of witnesses, let us lay aside every weight, and the sin which so easily ensnares us, and let us run with endurance the race that is set before us, looking unto Jesus, the author and finisher (perfecter) of our faith, who for the joy that was set before Him endured the cross..."*

The Amplified Bible says the finisher brings our faith to maturity and perfection! We are so thankful He is doing that in our lives. I pray when people look at me they see HIS reflection as He continues to work and perfect my life.

I told those tumors from day one that they were trespassing in this body and they would go. The work is not yet finished, but we are seeing God perform His Word. His is Faithful. A journey is not one big leap, but a process, a step by step process!

Follow up

April 2016: I have been off of chemotherapy for nearly six months now. After recent tests the doctor advises that we restart chemotherapy next week. The liver and the stomach lining have shown tumor growth. The journey is long, but Jesus never gets weary. I will continue to lean on Him. I will continue to trust Him. These developments do not change His plans for me. There is no doubt in me whatsoever. I also know that I will love and trust Him regardless of what the reports say. He has handled this step by step and will not stop now!

So, there we are. One day at a time. Step by step. The journey continues. I am grateful and full of hope. Please continue to pray, as I know you will.

God is good and He does all things well!

About the Author

I grew up in small town Texas. Life was very uneventful and routine. One of the most exciting things in our town was when the high school football team would make a run to the state play offs. Everyone knows everyone in Silsbee, TX and most of us are related in one way or another. I grew up with an amazing family: Mama, Daddy, and three older brothers. I am the baby, and the only girl. I grew up in church and was raised to love God. At an early age I felt the Lord call me into missions. Little did I know that I would one day live many years in Africa with my husband and youngest daughter.

My husband, Jerry and I have been married for over 21 years now. He is the most perfect example of Jesus I have ever seen. I have two daughters, Haeley and Arden. Haeley is married to a wonderful, Godly man, Joel. Arden is in college. We have one daughter from Kenya currently living with us, and other family in Kenya who we still love and support and pray one day will be with us here in the states. We have an amazing life. We are so blessed.

My very first priority in life is to share Jesus Christ with everyone. My husband and I are both licensed and ordained ministers and have devoted ourselves entirely to sharing the Good News. Secondly, my desire is to see people live at the level of victory that Christ has already given to us. We do that by daily applying the Word and speaking life to our situations. I want to help guide people into the Presence of The Lord where real change takes place.

BOOK DEBORAH

Deborah speaks at engagements world-wide. She loves to share her relationship with Christ and the insight she has to live victoriously every day. She is an overcomer and loves to teach others how to overcome! She has a down home style that is relaxing, and humorous, while at the same time challenging. She is a no-nonsense woman with a gift to stir up your Faith and motivate you to do more, be more, and love more. Her story is fitting for your church, women's meeting, and even corporate settings. The message is encouraging and uplifting to everyone who hears. Deborah is currently scheduling speaking engagements and may be reached at daysofelisha@yahoo.com

CONNECT ONLINE!

Facebook: www.facebook.com/deborahss1
Twitter: www.twitter.com/daysofelisha
Instagram: www.instagram.com/deborahsanfordsmith

Days of Elisha Ministries, USA
P O Box 1756
Silsbee, TX 77656
USA
daysofelisha@yahoo.com
www.daysofelisha.org

Made in the USA
San Bernardino, CA
05 August 2016